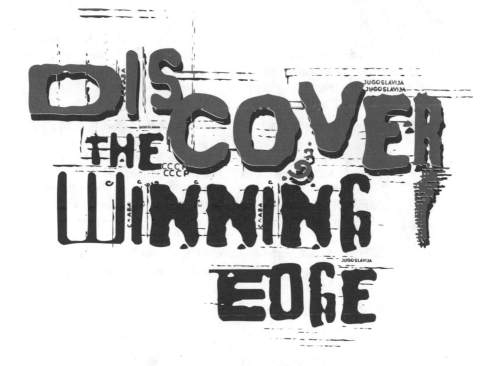

DISCOVER THE WINNING EDGE

William Mitchell
Jerry Pounds

LIFEWAY
Nashville, Tennessee

Dr. William Mitchell is a leading national authority on personal and family development. He is the founder and president of The Power of Positive Students International Foundation. Holding a doctorate in education from the University of Alabama, Dr. Mitchell has served with distinction in a variety of academic positions including teacher, coach, principal, superintendent of schools, and assistant professor. As a college student, his life was forever changed because of his involvement in the Baptist Student Union. He not only wrote a book about giant-killers *Winning in the Land of Giants,* in this book he shows us how to slay them on campus and *Discover the Winning Edge* in life.

Dr. Jerry Pounds is the author of *Hormones in Tennis Shoes* and co-author of *Christian Self-esteem: Parenting by Grace.* He is a native of Louisiana. He is the Associate Pastor for Administration at First Baptist Church, Spartanburg, SC. He formerly served as Associate Professor at New Orleans Baptist Theological Seminary in New Orleans, LA. He holds degrees from Samford University (B.A), New Orleans Baptist Seminary (M.R.E.), and Vanderbilt University (Ed.D.). He served as the editor of LIFE courses for the Sunday School Board of the Southern Baptist Convention. He is married to Bayne, and has two children, Rebecca and Jerry.

Editor: Art Herron
Production Specialist: Heather Platt
Graphic Designer: Bob Redden

0-7673-3178-8

Contents

Introduction

God creates every person uniquely. We are created for a special purpose. God has a plan for each of us when we are created. But, very few know this. For those who know this reality, few are courageous enough to respond to God's call for their lives. The one thing which keeps us from achieving our potential is "grasshopper mentality." Overcoming "grasshopper mentality" directs us to God's promises with the challenge to act upon them. *Discover the Winning Edge* is based on basic truths found in *Winning in the Land of Giants*.

Making the Most of This Workbook
The book you are reading is interactive. In each chapter and each day's study you are asked to consider a case study at the beginning of every day, memorize a Scripture passage each week, complete each day's activities, make a commitment to act on what you have learned, dig deeper into God's Word and evaluate the content of each day's study in light of how it applies to your life as a college student.

Also, throughout the book you will find red sidebars on the left. These indicate opportunities for you to dialogue with the authors, think about a truth you have discovered, or examine how you are doing as you discover the winning edge in your life. The case study at the beginning of each session can be used for a discussion starter if you are reading the book as part of a group.

Each chapter is illustrated through the use of an icon. Each week is represented by a different icon. These icons are intended to help you understand the content through a visual means. At the end of the book, you will find all six icons. You may want to photocopy these icons and place them in your room, notebook, backpack...someplace where you will see them each day. They will affirm your importance to God.

You are about to embark on an exciting journey as you *Discover the Winning Edge* for your life!

Developing Powerful Positive Thoughts

Day 1: Obedience to God

Principle: Christ-controlled thoughts overcome inferiority feelings.

Verse to Memorize This Week: "Finally, brethren, whatever things are true, whatever things are noble, whatever things are just, whatever things are pure, whatever things are lovely, whatever things are of good report, if there is any virtue and if there is anything praiseworthy--meditate on these things."--Philippians 4:8

> Jodi came to college on her own. Most of her friends chose the popular state school, but because of a specific major, she decided to attend a small, private college far from home. Her first few weeks were rough. She knew no one. Her actions identified her as an "outsider." She even felt that her looks were different than the others. Jodi didn't really feel that she measured up to those around her.

Have you viewed yourself as inferior to someone else while in college? We all have felt this to some degree. This perception of inferiority can cause us to possess a "grasshopper mentality."

JUGOSLAVIJA

Introduction

What is "grasshopper mentality?" Maybe you think if you have grasshopper mentality you will look like the grasshopper in the picture on the next page. The idea for this term is actually found in the Bible. In the Old Testament a man named Moses sent a group of spies to check out a place called Canaan which was known as "The Land of Promise." They did as they were told, and for 40 days, they surveyed the land. Caleb and Joshua, two of the spies, couldn't believe how beautiful it was. When they returned and gave their report, they said "It truly flows with milk and honey." All the cities in the land were also heavily fortified. Caleb said, "Let us go up at once and take possession, for we are well able to overcome it." Joshua agreed with him. The other 10 spies had another view. When they saw the people, they thought they would be stronger because they were

"of great stature." In fact, the spies thought the people were giants. And, upon seeing them they commented, "we were like grasshoppers in our own sight, and so we were in their sight" (Num. 13:33). And as is so often the case, in this instance the grasshopper mentality prevailed and the people did not take the land.

> "...like grasshoppers in our own sight, and so we were in their sight."

Get the picture? When the spies saw people who appeared to be giants, they felt they were no match for them. Their feelings of inferiority prevented them from claiming what God had planned for them.

Why do you think Moses was so easily swayed by the report given by the intimidated spies? Perhaps because he had already chosen to operate from a grasshopper mentality earlier in his life. Read the account given in Exodus 4:1-31.

What excuses did Moses have for not obeying God?
(Check all that apply.)
- ❑ He did not want to obey God.
- ❑ He did not hear God speaking.
- ❑ He did not want to disobey his mother.

What did Moses miss out on when he failed God's quiz on obedience? _____
_____

As you read Exodus 4:1-31, did you discover that
- Moses continues to deal with his feelings of inferiority.
- Moses continues to make excuses to God why he can't do what God wants him to do.
- God continues to communicate to Moses how He will provide.
- God reveals His character and His confidence in Moses.

Circle any statement above which speaks to current needs in your own life. Are you at the point of discovering the winning edge? You don't have to answer just yet.

The end result for Moses was that the children of Israel wondered in the wilderness for 40 years, intimidated by the people of Canaan, until all of those who had grasshopper mentality had died. Joshua and Caleb alone were allowed the privilege of going into the

promised land and eventually conquering it, as they had believed all along they were destined to do.

Just as God provided for Moses, God provides for you. In the space below, write down the name of a person who has been a blessing in your life. Describe the ways that person has been a blessing to you because of his or her faithfulness and obedience to God.

In Deuteronomy 11:26-28 you read how God spoke to the people of Israel about blessings and curses. Receiving God's blessings or curses depends on one's relationship to God. Not only did Moses have to discover this, but the whole nation of Israel had to discover this principle as well. Is it a lesson for your generation? In what way can you show obedience to God? Write down one way you can show obedience to God under each heading below.

In relationships with friends?

On campus in the disciplines in your life, such as your studies?

With other Christians?

To God?

If we obey the commandments of God, we can become a _____. If we choose to do things our own way, to trust in ourselves rather than God, or by accepting an inferior position, we will lose out on the blessing God has for us.

Bryce Paup, linebacker for the Buffalo Bills, could have fallen into a grasshopper mentality mode. The 6'5," 247-pounder played his 1994 season with the Green Bay Packers. Even though he made the Pro Bowl at the end of that season, the Packers did not make a serious offer to keep him on the team. Despite his success, Paup still played in the shadow of perennial Pro Bowl lineman Reggie White.

"I was kind of bitter," Bryce admitted. "The door (in Green Bay) was shut in my face. But I prayed about it, and this is where God wanted me. So, I just had to give it (bitterness) up because this is where He wanted me."

Not bad for someone who at the end of the 1995 season was named Defensive Player of the Year by AP, UPI, and others, chosen NFL Alumni's Linebacker of the Year, and named Most Valuable Player of the AFC by the NFL Players Association.[1]

Bryce Paup—Moses—You...all may have something in common. Seeking to find one's place in this world but plagued with feelings of inferiority and self-doubt. Yet, in each of the illustrations you have seen how God worked in their lives. Check all which apply when you think about God working in your life. God will

❑ find me an unwilling person.

❑ discover many weaknesses in my life.

❑ see me as a victim of grasshopper mentality in many things I have tried to do.

❑ find a person who desires to discover the winning edge in life.

❑ work in my life to help me be more positive.

If you are like me you could check each one. Now consider Moses again. Not quite yet on God's Pro Bowl team, he could have avoided that grasshopper mentality if he had listened to God rather than himself. How about you? Are you listening to others more than to God? We do not need to struggle with feeling intimidated by people or situations. It is possible to live as Philippians 4:13 admonishes: "I can do all things through Christ who strengthens me."

Part of the solution comes in recognizing the problem and choosing to confront it. You must also take active steps on a daily basis toward replacing attitudes of inferiority, insecurity, and inadequacy with positive beliefs and behaviors.

Today I will demonstrate obedience to God by

_____

_____

_____

Steps to Discovering the Winning Edge
1. We all have experienced the feeling of inferiority.
2. We become a blessing when we obey God.
3. Christ gives us strength to do all things.

BACK 2 U

Think about Jodi again for a moment. Is she close to discovering the winning edge? If Jodi were a friend of yours, how could you help her discover the winning edge based on what you learned today?

[1]Bentz, Rob. "Paup & Circumstance." *Sports Spectrum*, November 1996, 18-19.

Day 2: Chosen by God

Principle: Christ-controlled thoughts overcome inferiority feelings.

Tony grew up in a Christian home. You could say that he was one of the key leaders when it came to participating in the college ministry at church. Tony could always be counted on, even though he was a little rowdy at times. Everyone felt Tony was a Christian. Why would he attend so many activities if he was not one? The fact is that no one could remember if Tony ever made a public profession at church. Looking back now, he was always around...

God is not interested in appearances. He is interested in how our hearts look. You and I may judge people by how they look, but God looks at the heart. Let's examine the life of David, the giant slayer, God's chosen one.

As you read 1 Samuel 16 and 17 you will discover how God works.

Imagine yourself the youngest of eight boys in a family. Low man on the totem pole. The baby of the family. The little kid. The last to be chosen. David grew up overlooked and probably ignored, except for the fact that one day a man had come into his life and said, "This is the one!" That man had been the prophet Samuel, who had come to Jesse's house at God's order and anointed David with oil in front of his brothers. David would be Israel's future king--God's chosen replacement after Saul failed to live up to God's standards for kingship.

Look carefully at 1 Samuel 16:7. Do you think David was chosen because of his: (check all that you feel apply)
- ❑ a) looks
- ❑ b) size
- ❑ c) heart

Take a closer look at 1 Samuel 17:26-37. What negative statements did others use to try to discourage David from taking on Goliath? List some below.

David certainly wasn't a giant of a man in his brothers' eyes when he arrived in their military camp one day at the request of his father. In fact, when he arrived, it was Goliath who was strutting up and down the valley. We have no reason to believe that David is a giant killer.

David wasn't yet a winner in the land of giants. However, as you consider the Scripture passage, do you believe David was thinking like a winner?
❑ Yes   ❑ No   Give one reason for your answer.

No one was willing to stand up to the challenge. No one...except David himself. "Let no man's heart fail because of him; your servant will go and fight with this Philistine."

Examine 1 Samuel 17:45-53 and put down one reason why you think David was able to triumph over Goliath.

David knew who he was. He was a shepherd, the son of _____, an Israelite, a chosen child of _____, and a man anointed by _____. He knew the Spirit of the Lord was with him. He also believed that God was on the side of Israel. David knew that he was somebody and that he was associated with somebody bigger than Goliath.

The person who is a winner in the land of giants inevitably carries these same traits as David.

As seen in David, a giant slayer exhibits these four traits:
- He is in the Lord--a child of God.
- She has a divine destiny--chosen by the Lord.
- God is greater than any giant.
- In order to slay the giant, she must be herself--have confidence in herself.

Look at the four traits above. Place an exclamation point (!) beside the trait(s) you have mastered and a question mark (?) beside the trait(s) you struggle with now.

Recall a time when you stood up with a strong conviction. Who or what was your giant? What giant-slayer traits did you exhibit in that situation?

_____
_____
_____
_____
_____
_____

After David volunteered to face Goliath, his actions were noteworthy. Taking a stone, David slung it with great force. He found his mark. Giant slayers today also exhibit these traits of David.

Giant slayers:
- hit their mark
- run toward their enemy
- finish the job
- shout back positively

Rewrite these phrases in the correct chronological order.

1_____when the world shouts
  negatively at them,
2_____, seeing them as challenges
  to be conquered.
3_____, doing what they know to do
  with all their ability.
4_____, completely and definitively.

Getting to the point where you think like a giant slayer is a process. It takes time. We are often given opportunities to face smaller giants before we face larger ones. David had developed courage over time.

Where are you spiritually? How has God prepared you to tackle the challenges you are currently facing as a college student?

_____
_____
_____

David was chosen by God because of his heart. How is your heart? The first step in the process of growth is to know Him. Decide now to know God. Follow this simple outline:

a) Admit that you are a sinner (Rom. 3:10-12, 23).
b) Realize the penalty for your sin (Rom. 6:23).
c) Acknowledge payment God made for your sin (Rom. 5:8).
d) Confess Jesus as your Lord and ask God to save you (Rom. 10:9, 10, 13).

After reading what the Bible says about knowing and choosing Jesus, are you willing to make that decision now? If so, pray this simple prayer. God understands your heart.

Dear God:

I know you love me. I realize that I am a sinner and that I have not lived the way you would want me to live. I believe that Jesus died on the cross for me, and He was raised from death to provide forgiveness and eternal life. I ask that you save me as I turn from my sins. I place my faith in you and receive you as my Lord and Savior. Give me the strength to live for you. Thank you for saving me and giving me eternal life. I pray this in Jesus' name. Amen.

If you prayed this prayer, share your decision with your leader or a Christian friend. We are encouraged to grow in faith, grow in our ability to care for others, and grow to become fully mature in the Lord. As we grow, the Holy Spirit transforms, changes, and renews our minds.

Pray and ask God to help you identify what giant-slayer traits He desires to build into your life.

I will affirm the spiritual reality that I am chosen by God as I

_____

_____

_____

Steps to Discovering the Winning Edge
1. Man looks at the outward appearance, but God looks at the heart.
2. Trust God when facing problems.
3. Before God can choose to use us, we must choose Him as our Lord and Savior.

Back 2 U
Think about Tony. Is he close to discovering the winning edge?
Based on what you learned today, if Tony were your friend, how could you help him discover that Christ-controlled thoughts are more than just being active in church?

Day 3: Faith in God

Principle: Christ-controlled thoughts overcome inferiority feelings.

Catherine was the one you could always count on. Being in college did not prevent her from leading in prayer or guiding Bible discussion in a small group in the dorm. Catherine's enthusiasm to learn more about God's ways was contagious. Other women in the dorm wanted to discover her secret as she displayed the ways of God in her daily life. It was obvious that her faith was real and dynamic.

Read Numbers 14:1-9 and Joshua 14:6-12.

Before going any further, write a one-sentence definition of faith.

_____

_____

_____

_____

_____

_____

Do you think by your definition you have faith? ❏ Yes ❏ No

Let's examine one man's faith in God.

Although we may think of David as the famous giant slayer of the Bible, the first giant slayer was actually Caleb. Caleb was one of the two spies who went into Canaan and returned with a faithful word. As far as we know, Caleb and Joshua were the only two men who survived the 40 years of wandering in the wilderness and were allowed to enter the promised land. Their faith in God's ability to give them the land never wavered, and neither did their obedience in following the Lord.

After much of the land of Canaan had been taken by the Israelites under the leadership of Joshua, the children of Judah came to Gilgal. Caleb made a bold request of Joshua. He asked that the mountain of the giants, (the Anakim,) be given to him as an inheritance. Caleb was still ready and willing to take on the giants. He hadn't wavered in his belief that God wanted His people to possess Canaan. He didn't use any excuses. He wasn't college age. At age 85, he considered himself able to defeat the giants. Joshua blessed Caleb and gave him Hebron as an inheritance for his family.

13

Caleb took on the giant of the giants. He captured Hebron and turned it into his own city. Note a giant principle about giant-slaying thinking. Do you want to demonstrate your faith in God while in college? Understand that *the victory of one winner very often inspires another winner*. Caleb's victory over the Anakim inspired David, who inspired the entire army of Saul to pursue the Philistines and win the war. If you want to start thinking like a winner in college, associate with others who also embrace a can-do, we-can-take-the-mountain, God-is-on-our-side attitude. These students are on your campus. Are you one of them at this point in your life? Maybe? Maybe not!

As the apostle Paul wrote to the Romans, "If God is for us, who can be against us?" (Rom. 8:31). If we find giants on the campus who are coming against us God will be on our side. Who can withstand God's protection and provisions?

Caleb demonstrated faith. Reread the definition of faith you wrote. How has your definition of faith changed over the years?
from childhood to adolescence? _____
_____
_____

from adolescence to young adulthood?_____
_____
_____

Faith in God––the Driving Force Behind Being Used by God
Shelly Stokes is one such example. Shelly learned to play softball in her hometown of Carmichael, California. She was good enough to then play at Fresno State. Little did Shelly know that she would make history by playing in the first-ever U.S. Olympic Softball Team for the 1996 Olympic Games in Atlanta. Like all of the athletes, the road to the Games involved years of training and hard work.

Shelly's role during the Olympic Games was more than just being a catcher. Not playing the final two games because of a change in rotation, Shelly became an unselfish team player who encouraged her teammates with a positive attitude. When not playing softball, Shelly modeled her faith in God by leading a Bible study with several of her teammates. The gold medal was her goal, but serving God was her real life's motivation. "I knew I wouldn't have been a good witness if I had been selfish about not playing. I think I have the respect of my teammates because I stand by my faith."[1]

In the Bible, the writer of Hebrews identified numerous examples of those who placed their faith in God. Check out Hebrews 11. Wow! Jot down what was said about the faith of:

Enoch _____

Noah _____

Abraham _____

Sarah _____

Based on what you read about Catherine, Shelly, and the heroes of faith in Hebrews 11, identify some elements of faith: (check those which apply)

❑ contagious   ❑ is real
❑ creates action   ❑ listens to God
❑ is enduring   ❑ believes a promise
❑ lasts for a lifetime   ❑ knows mother is always right

One more time, think about your earlier definition of faith. In light of the examples given in this study, has your definition changed? If so, how?

Now define "faith" in one or two words.

_____

_____

Faith can be understood as
      Forsaking
      All
      I
      Trust
      Him

Today, in these areas of my life I will pray for more faith:

_____

_____

_____

_____

_____

_____

15

Steps to Discovering the Winning Edge
1. God desires that we place our faith in Him.
2. Our faith in God is our true driving force in being used by God.
3. Without faith it is impossible to please God.

Back 2 U
How do you feel Catherine displayed faith? Is she close to knowing
the winning edge in her life?
What can you do on campus to be an example of faith to others
as they search for the winning edge?
Who is an example of faith to you on campus now?

[1]Gretzinger, Molly. "Atlanta Bravery." *Sports Spectrum*,
November 1996, 10-11.

Day 4: Thoughts and Behavior
Principle: Christ-controlled thoughts overcome inferiority feelings.

Tanya had the maturity to balance her work load with her school responsibilities. She maintained As and Bs in all of her classes in spite of her involvement in a service sorority as well as an active social life. Then one day at work, Tanya's boss informed her that she would have to start working all day on Saturday and take her turn during the Sunday shift. Tanya needed the money but not these extra burdens.

The Chinese symbol for the word *crisis* actually has two interpretations. It can be interpreted as "opportunity" or "problem." In fact, when you experience a crisis you can respond to it either as an opportunity or as a problem. One approach is positive and the other negative. In many situations, the attitude in which you approach a challenge primarily determines whether you succeed or fail.

This section deals with thoughts and behavior. No matter what, when, or where something happens to you, it will affect your thoughts and behavior. To illustrate the point, describe a time recently when you experienced a crisis. Did you view it as an opportunity or a problem? Respond in the space below.

Opportunity—why?

Problem—why?

All of our battles against circumstances and situations that are potentially defeating must be fought on a daily basis in the arena of one's thought life. The war itself may have been going on for some time, and may continue for days, weeks, months, and perhaps even years into the future. It is in the battle of the day that we must face and defeat our enemies of fear, discouragement, and failure.

List a fear, discouragement, or failure that you face daily as a student.

_____

_____

_____

What we think, we become. Scripture tells us that "as he thinks in his heart, so is he" (Prov. 23:7). Consider the power that our thoughts have on our physical condition. Remember trying to avoid some unpleasant situation (such as a test), telling yourself over and over again that you didn't feel well. Before long, you really didn't feel well at all!

17

Physicians will tell us that there is a definite link between an impact of faith and a positive attitude on a physical disease. Medical science has discovered that every thought we think produces a chemical in our bodies. Negative, worrisome thinking produces a chemically-unhealthy atmosphere for our cells while positive, loving thoughts create the chemically-happy environment our cells need to do their best work of keeping us healthy. On the other hand, positive thinking has been shown to release endorphins in the brain, which are the chemicals associated with a feeling of joy and a sense of well-being. These endorphins even block physical pain in the body.

Much has been written in the Bible concerning the struggle in our minds between negative and positive emotions and feelings. As believers, one's struggles do not go away or disappear for a while.

Below is a list of Scriptures. Read each of the passages. On the lines beside each reference, rewrite the verse(s) in your own words. Reread each Scripture a few times before creating your own translation.

2 Corinthians 10:3-5 _____

_____

Philippians 2:5 _____

_____

Ephesians 4:23 _____

_____

Philippians 4:8 _____

_____

James 2:12 _____

_____

Would you like to win your battles and struggles? This week's memory verse, Philippians 4:8, provides additional instruction on how to win the ongoing struggles in your life. In the space below, try to write out Philippians 4:8 from memory. If not, refer to your Bible and write the verse in the space below.

_____

_____

Our real challenge in facing battles each day is to decide how to think about them. Our first and foremost task is to take control of our thoughts.

Consider these two plans of action:

PLAN 1: Disperse it.
A technique used in tackling scientific problems is to break down a problem into its component parts and then to work at each part until an answer is reached.

As the component problems are solved, the big problem is also solved. This principle holds true for all of life. One of the most effective things a person can do about what seems to be an overwhelming problem is to attempt to break it down into its smaller component problems and then to deal with the smaller issues one at a time.

In the pie shape, write in each slice of the pie a situation or problem you need to work through.

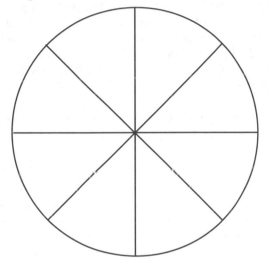

When you look upon all of the pieces in this pie, life can become overwhelming. Instead, address each situation, one at a time. You will soon find confidence in working through each manageable problem.

PLAN 2: Reverse it.
Seek out the positive. No situation or circumstance is 100 percent bad. There is always some glimmer of hope, some ray of light. Recognize negativity for what it is—a distraction from a positive solution. Dismiss the negativity. Of course, you do not ignore the problem in hopes that it will go away. To the contrary! Disposing of the negative thought means facing the problem *and* facing your negative response. It involves making a conscious decision that the negative response will do nothing to solve the problem, and in that light, refusing to dwell on the negative and turning instead to the positive. Only you can reverse the way you feel about a problem.

Go back to the fear, discouragement, or failure that you identified earlier. What are some glimmers of hope you can find in this situation? Record your thoughts in the margin of this page.

19

The story is told of an avid duck hunter who was in the market for a new bird dog. His search ended when he found a dog that would walk on water to retrieve a duck. Shocked by his discovery, the man wondered how he would break the news to his hunting friends. He was sure that no one would believe him.

The hunter decided to invite a buddy with him to see the phenomenon for himself. The two hunters made their way to the blind the next morning and waited. When the ducks flew nearby, the hunters shouldered their guns and fired. The dog responded by running across the water and retrieving a bird. The hunter's friend remained silent. He didn't say a word about the amazing dog. On the drive home, the hunter asked his friend, "Did you notice anything unusual about my new dog?" "I sure did," responded the friend. "He can't swim."

We can laugh at this little story, but the truth remains that many people are like that hunter's friend. They just hate to say the positive thing.

Today I will think more positively about myself and one other person which will impact how I relate to that person. List one person and what you will try to do. _____

_____

_____

_____

_____

_____

Steps to Discovering the Winning Edge
1. Every crisis can be an opportunity rather than a problem.
2. What we think, we become.
3. Bring every thought into captivity to the obedience of Christ.

Back 2 U
Think for a moment about Tanya's situation. How do you feel the change in her schedule can affect her negatively?
Based on your study of today's Scriptures, what advice could you offer her which might help her overcome these negative feelings?
When you have positive feelings in situations, do you feel you are close to discovering the winning edge in your life?

Day 5: Choosing the Thought

Principle: Christ-controlled thoughts overcome inferiority feelings.

Brent has been dealing with feelings of low self-esteem since arriving on campus. In high school, he was never the popular kid and was often chosen last for any team. He often replays in his mind over and over the words, "You can't do it, you'll only fail." Brent wants a way to escape from this paralyzing thought. Right now, his only option seems to be that he will flunk out of school.

Beyond positive thinking is positive doing. It's not enough to think the positive. You must move beyond that to do the positive. For example, as a college student you hear repeatedly about the principle of honesty and how it is right for a college student to be honest. However, it is not until you choose to act out honesty, to make the honest choice, to exhibit the honest behavior, that the real benefits of honesty are realized in your life.

Our greatest challenge is not only to think positively but also to respond and act in a positive manner, regardless of the circumstances. Both our thinking positively and our acting positively begin with our making a choice to think and act in this manner.

What is most difficult when you are called upon to make a choice to act in a positive manner? Is it making the choice? _____

_____

The apostle Paul exhorted the Christians at Philippi to dwell on positive thoughts. Open your Bible and examine Philippians 4:8-9.

What does Paul list as the six "whatevers"? Complete the sentence below.

Whatever is _____ , _____ , _____ ,

_____ , _____ , _____ .

Paul also states that if anything is _____ or

_____ , to think about those things.

Paul further encourages believers to put into practice that which we have learned, received, heard, and have seen, in him.

List someone who you have looked up to over the years who has put his or her faith into action?_____

_____

21

What Christlike qualities did this person exhibit? (List these qualities beside each of the boxes with one or two words.)

❏   ❏
❏   ❏
❏   ❏
❏   ❏

What does Paul say in Philippians 4:8-9 will happen to the person who thinks "about such things"? _____

_____

Would you like to make more positive choices? Below are two exercises you might try as you make a choice for the positive in your life right now.

Exercise A: Separating the Positive and the Negative

Take two sheets of paper. Title one "Negative" and the other "Positive." On the sheet titled "Negative," write three negative thoughts that you think frequently. They may be thoughts about yourself, another person, a situation, your future, or your past. On the sheet titled "Positive," write down three positive attributes or habits that you want to acquire or develop. Now tear up the sheet labeled "Negative" and throw away all the pieces of paper. *Consider yourself to be finished with those thoughts.* Take the sheet headed "Positive," and post it some place––perhaps on the wall at your desk, in a binder you open often, in a favorite book or magazine, or next to the phone. If you have a roommate you might even have him or her read over your positive thoughts and join you in this exercise. Remind yourself frequently of the positive attributes or habits you want to develop. The more you put those thoughts into your mind, the more likely you are to act on them. The more you act on them, the more they will be habitual to you. About 95 percent of what we do in a day is out of habit. Make your habits positive!

Exercise B: Replacing Negative Input

Think a moment about information that you have gained in the last 24 hours. Then write down several of the most negative things you have seen, heard, or experienced.

1.
2.
3.

What feelings do you have when you think about those things? (Check those words listed below which best describe your overall feelings during these times.)

   ❏ frustration   ❏ turmoil
   ❏ bitterness   ❏ anxiety

❑ disappointment   ❑ fear
❑ stress   ❑ other _____

What can you do to eliminate the negative from your life? Do you need to turn off the television set for awhile? Do you need to listen to a different type of music? Do you need to find new friends on campus...and even at church? Do you need to tell a negative-speaking friend that you want to discuss positive things?

Now, write down several positive things you've heard or experienced in the last 24 hours.
1.
2.
3.

What happens when you think about those things? Do you find yourself smiling, feeling contentment and joy, anticipating tomorrow? Describe your feelings below. What images come to mind that make the difference?

You can choose to be a part of the small percentage of people who take control of their lives—including the thought life of their minds and emotions of their hearts. Choose what you will take into your life and what you will reject.

When you hear a positive comment about yourself—even if it's one you have to voice to yourself in the mirror! Choose to focus on that thought.

The best choice is consistent, slow, steady, daily improvement. This will develop the positive in your mind and heart.

Make these choices on a daily basis:
- Choose to read what builds you up as a person and makes you have more hope.
- Choose to listen to messages that cause you to love yourself and others more generously and genuinely.
- Choose to engage in activities that strengthen you mentally, physically, and emotionally.

Consider your activities during the last week. What negative and positive choices did you make in regard to what you read, listened to, and did?

Consider negative messages that were sent to these famous people:
- Beethoven's music teacher said, "As a composer, he is hopeless."
- Thomas Edison's teacher told him he was unable to learn.
- Caruso's music teacher told him that, he had "no voice at all."
- Louis Pasteur was given a rating of "mediocre" in chemistry at Royal College.
- A newspaper editor fired Walt Disney from his staff because he had "no good ideas."
- Henry Ford was once evaluated as "showing no promise."

Each of these people refused to allow negative bombs to go off in their lives and destroy their desire, ambition, creativity, or willingness to keep trying.

Are you allowing negative messages to stifle your growth? Pray and ask God to help you respond to positive comments.

Today, I will choose positive thoughts by_____

_____

_____

_____

_____

Steps to Discovering the Winning Edge
1. Beyond positive thinking is positive doing.
2. Our greatest challenge is to respond and act in a positive manner, regardless of the circumstances.
3. Make the choice on a daily basis to feed on the positive in your mind and heart.

Back 2 U
Can you identify with Brent?
What will it take for him to discover the winning edge?
What do you feel Brent needs to develop a strong self-esteem?
What is the best thing you have learned from this session
about the importance of knowing the power of the winning edge?

Experiencing a Second Chance

Day 1: Words of Value

Principle: God gives second chances to those who trust Him.

Verse to Memorize This Week: "If we confess our sins, He is faithful and just to forgive us our sins and to cleanse us from all unrighteousness." — 1 John 1:9

> Jessica was very particular, especially in how she looked and what she wore. In some ways, she was the fashion trendsetter at her school. No one could accuse her of being vain, she just always seemed to know what to wear for the occasion. Because of this, Jessica was not prepared to hear the words of her roommate when she said, "Jessica, I love your hair. But why did you cut it so short?"

"Friendly fire" is a military term used to describe the results when aircraft, military installations, and valued personnel are destroyed inadvertently by their own armed forces. Sometimes the error is caused by mechanical or technological malfunction. Very often, however, tragedy stems from human error. In those cases, the victims are not only the ones who are killed by the friendly fire but, psychologically, those who have caused the death and destruction.

Many times we produce friendly fire by the words we use, as we saw in the case study involving Jessica. Most friendly fire is not intentional. It occurs because people pulling the trigger or pushing the buttons––psychologically, emotionally, and relationally speaking––are unaware of the damage they are doing to another person. In other cases, people are simply careless with their tongues and the expression of their opinions.

We are all guilty of friendly fire. Following are six statements that describe the kinds of careless words and behavior we sometimes produce. As you read each statement, examine your life. Consider whether you are

issuing friendly fire in what you say and do. Then circle the word that is most appropriate for you in response to each statement.

1. Negative and Exclusive Statements
This occurs when we say things that make people feel that they are not a part of the team or that their contribution to a team effort doesn't count. I do this...

Never   Rarely   Sometimes   Often   Always

2. Negative Conditioning
A person repeatedly plants negative thoughts into the mind of another person. Unfortunately, we can inflict this type of friendly fire upon ourselves. The fact is that most of the self-defeating put-downs we hear are self spoken or self thought. I do this...

Never   Rarely   Sometimes   Often   Always

3. Negative Reinforcement
Sometimes people find fault with what others do and never look for the good in them or their accomplishments. A person might do five things right and only one thing wrong, but the person pulling the friendly-fire trigger notices only the one thing that was done wrong. I do this...

Never   Rarely   Sometimes   Often   Always

4. Negative Climate
The communication, conversations, and media messages that most of us encounter on a daily basis are filled with negative messages. Some have estimated that 80 percent of the messages we hear in a day are negative. I experience this...

Never   Rarely   Sometimes   Often   Always

5. Negative Self-Talk Passed On
When we engage in negative self-talk, others frequently hear us mumbling, and our negative attitudes and words spread to the point where others unconsciously begin mumbling negative things to themselves. I do this...

Never   Rarely   Sometimes   Often   Always

6. Negative Modeling
People frequently model nonverbal behaviors that cause others to feel inferior or intimidated. I do this...

Never   Rarely   Sometimes   Often   Always

When you look at your circles, how did you do? Would you see yourself as being a person who speaks words of value? Or can you see room for major improvement? Do not despair, God's Word will help you to continue making changes to your verbal habits.

Take a look at the Scriptures below. Indicate by checking the appropriate box(es) whether the Scripture described an **action** you can take to use your tongue for good; a **benefit** from using your tongue for good; a **negative consequence** of using your tongue for bad; or a **warning** against using your tongue for bad (some verses include more than one item). Then in the space that is provided, write out the specific action, benefit, consequence, or warning mentioned in Scripture.

Psalm 141:3 --*"Set a guard, O Lord, over my mouth; keep watch over the door of my lips."*
❑ action   ❑ benefit   ❑ negative consequence   ❑ warning

_____

_____

Proverbs 15:4 --*"A wholesome tongue is a tree of life, but perverseness in it breaks the spirit."*
❑ action   ❑ benefit   ❑ negative consequence   ❑ warning

_____

_____

Proverbs 24:28 --*"Do not be a witness against your neighbor without cause, for would you deceive with your lips?"*
❑ action   ❑ benefit   ❑ negative consequence   ❑ warning

_____

_____

Matthew 12:36 --*"But I say to you that for every idle word men may speak, they will give account of it in the day of judgment."*
❑ action   ❑ benefit   ❑ negative consequence   ❑ warning

_____

_____

James 1:26 --*"If anyone among you thinks he is religious, and does not bridle his tongue but deceives his own heart, this one's religion is useless."*
❑ action   ❑ benefit   ❑ negative consequence   ❑ warning

Now look up Ephesians 4:29-32. Use your Bible, reference notes, or a Bible concordance to answer the following questions.

What are some examples of "unwholesome talk"?_____

_____

_____

What is meant by "building others up"?_____

_____

Positive words go a long way in building others up. When we share these words with others, we are building them up on the inside and helping to create something positive in their lives. Consider these, then add your own:

- "Way to go!"
- "Congratulations!"

- "Thank you."
- "I am proud of you."

_____   _____

We also need to speak positive words to ourselves. Add your own to this list:

- "I did my best."
- "I am worthy."
- "I am somebody."

- "I am valuable to this group."
- "I am loved by God."
- "I am a child of God."

_____   _____

In spite of what we may hear from others, God desires us to keep the faith. Jane Albright-Dieterle is such an example. Head woman's basketball coach at the University of Wisconsin, Jane earned the 1995 Big Ten Coach of the Year Award. Success was obvious—ticket sales had been up, high ranking in the poles, several sell-out crowds, one of the leaders in attendance growth. But in spite of all her success, some residents of Madison, Wisconsin had called for her resignation because of her Christian witness. But instead of being defensive, Jane responded, "I feel that my approval has to be from the Lord and not really from man...As long as I feel like that's what the Lord wants me to do, I know that it's His battle and not mine, and He'll take care of it. When it gets hard, I think that's really the Lord driving me to my knees."[1]

When we value those around us, we increase their value. When we value those around us, they value themselves more. When we value those around us, our perspective about them changes.

Today, I will work at speaking words of value by _____
_____

Steps to Discovering the Winning Edge
1. What we say affects others negatively or positively.
2. God desires that our words be used to build others up.
3. When we value those around us, we increase their value.

Back 2 U
Do you think Jessica was a victim of friendly fire?
Think about a time when you were the victim. How did it feel?
How does this apply to discovering the winning edge?

[1]Flynn, Bev. "Sports People Who Lead By Example."
Sports Spectrum, December 1996, 15.

Day 2: Confession of the Heart

Principle: God gives second chances to those who trust Him.

Carson is not proud of all he has done since arriving at college. He often feels he lets others down who care for him. He has been tempted by more things than he could ever imagine. Shortly before entering college, Carson recommitted his life to Christ. He is far from being a perfect person but strives to be the person God wants him to be. Not a day goes by without Carson claiming the promise of 1 John 1:9. He gets a second chance every day.

How often have you entered a classroom, sat down for a lecture, and taken notes by way of a chalkboard? Then, the cycle begins again with new notes on a clean board. Starting over. Wiping the slate clean. Confession.

Second chances will come your way as you trust God.

In the box to the right, we find encouraging words from 1 John. Take a moment to memorize 1 John 1:9, this week's memory verse. Once you have memorized the verse, write it down.

> "If we confess our sins, He is faithful and just to forgive us our sins and to cleanse us from all unrighteousness."
> --1 John 1:9

_____

_____

_____

_____

It's up to us to receive His forgiveness and accept that His cleansing truly wipes out any old messages on our slate. Seeking and receiving God's forgiveness is the first step.

First John 1:9 speaks to seven key words for one who will discover the winning edge. Examine each word. Beside that word write down a word that means the same thing, but comes from everyday language.

Confess _____

Sins _____

Faithful _____

Just _____

Forgive _____

Cleanse _____

Unrighteousness _____

Were you able to match each word with a word that doesn't come from the Bible? Did you have difficulty finding a word that meant the same thing as the biblical word?

Which two words have you now gained a better understanding of by your comparison?

_____   _____

According to 1 John 1:9:

When can a Christian confess his or her sins? _____

_____
_____
_____
_____

What does God promise to do? _____

_____
_____
_____
_____

A New Promise

The words in 2 Corinthians 5:17 hold out great promise for a clean slate: "Therefore, if anyone is in Christ, he is a new creation; old things have passed away; behold, all things have become new."

What do you think the phrase "in Christ" means? Jot down a simple definition to express what you feel it means. _____

_____
_____
_____
_____
_____
_____

Telling Others

Outline your testimony by responding to these three questions:
1. What was your life like before receiving Christ?

2. What is your life like after receiving Christ?

3. What is Christ doing in your life now?

30

The former Notre Dame football coach, Lou Holtz, knows about second chances. Before coaching Notre Dame, Holtz coached at William and Mary, North Carolina State, the University of Arkansas, and the University of Minnesota. In each case, he inherited a losing team and wound up taking the team to a bowl game in his second year at the school. Holtz was given the opportunity to wipe the slate clean.

Holtz called a team meeting after Notre Dame lost the Cotton Bowl to Texas A & M in 1987. He gave what the players came to call, "The Perfection Speech." Holtz presented to his players a vision he had for their lives––how they would be perfect in the classroom, practice the best, and be perfect in their overall lives. He then asked all those in the room who wanted to win the national championship in 1988 to stand up. Everybody in the room stood. That set the turnaround, second-chance tone for Notre Dame, which did indeed win the 1988 college football championship.

Several things about Lou Holtz stand out. **First**, he factors God into his life. Lou Holtz doesn't attempt to realize his dreams or seize his second chances without turning to his Bible and to the Lord. **Second**, even in the face of a defeat, he sets a bigger goal––not only for himself but for his teams. **Third**, he pursues his goals with efforts and persistence. **Fourth**, he wants his players to have character, even more than he wants them to wear championship rings.

Do you find it hard to accept that someone is willing to wipe the slate clean in your life? Someone is ready to give you a second chance, willing to give you the opportunity to start over, but are you clutching to doubts and memories that keep you rooted in past failure? If so, through God's help and Scripture, you need to have your slate wiped clean.

Remember, God is always ready for you to respond. (Take a moment now to pray this prayer to God.) "OK, Lord, I will go with you on this. I choose to believe about myself what you believe about me."

Make a commitment now to start each day new.

In the statements below, circle at least one key word in each sentence that will help you remember how to start each day with a clean slate.
> • End each day by confessing your sins to God and accepting
>   His forgiveness into your life.
> • Greet the Lord each morning with a request that He guide and
>   guard your steps, confessing your need for
>   Him.
> • Expect something good to happen to you
>   all the day through.

Steps to Discovering the Winning Edge
1. Seeking and receiving God's forgiveness is the first step
in starting over.
2. Once we experience God's forgiveness, then we need
to forgive ourselves.
3. Only the Lord sees our full potential.

Back 2 U
How is Carson obtaining a second chance?
Is a second chance essential in order to discover the winning edge?
If you were Carson's best friend, would you be willing to share with him the
condition of your heart during a time of confession?
When was the last time you confessed before God?

Day 3: Forgiveness and Forgiven

Principle: God gives second chances to those who trust Him.

Vicki grew up in a small town which seemed to have churches located on every corner. Most of her friends attended church, but not the same one. Occasionally she would go with a friend, mostly for the fellowship. Vicki never personally responded to receive Christ in her life. She remembered hearing that God had a plan for her life, but she knew nothing of God's promise to forgive her sins. Vicki knew she had "done some things wrong in her life," but really didn't know what to do about them.

First John 1:9 reminds us that "if we confess our sins, He is faithful and just to forgive us our sins and to cleanse us from all unrighteousness." God stands willing and ready to forgive us of our sins and to cleanse us. Our confession of these sins must come first.

What God says, He will do. He is totally faithful, a keeper of His word. The apostle Paul wrote, "He who calls you is faithful, who also will do it" (1 Thess. 5:24). He also wrote, "God is faithful, by whom you were called into the fellowship of His Son, Jesus Christ our Lord" (1 Cor. 1:9). He is a God of His word.

Take a sheet of paper and list some of the wrong things you have done lately, things you have not asked God to forgive. After listing these, ask the Lord to forgive you. Claim 1 John 1:9. Then take this paper and crumple it up. Find a trash can and dump it. Symbolically, God has forgiven you. He wants you to experience forgiveness for wrongs which are sins. Not symbolically, but in reality!

What is the process we need to follow to experience authentic forgiveness?

The first step is asking God for forgiveness. You may have a package at the post office, but until you ask for it, you won't get it. The same is true for forgiveness. God has already planned for you to receive it. Now ask for it.

The second step we need to take is to forgive ourselves. That sounds easier than it is. For many people, it is not enough to say one time, "I won't let that bother me again" or "I forgive myself, and I will never think about this again."

Confession and forgiveness put us in a position to be used by God.

Read Judges 6:12-40 and Judges 7.

Gideon is an example of a man God forgave and then Gideon used his forgiveness to become a somebody. If you have read the Scripture, you know what God did through Gideon was fantastic.

Even when Gideon questioned God's ability, God did not hold that against Gideon. He was forgiven.

Consider for just a moment what would have happened if Gideon had stubbornly retained his old grasshopper mentality. How many more years would Israel have suffered under the Midianites?

Who would have earned Gideon's place in God's Word as an example of how God can forgive His people if they are only willing to obey Him and believe about themselves what He believes about them? Those who humbly turn to God and obey Him are forgiven and free do extraordinary things through God.

When we receive God's forgiveness, He puts us in the position to experience a second chance, another opportunity, a turnaround moment. He puts us into a sequence of experiences and events that results in victory for ourselves and for all of God's people.

What would have happened if Gideon had turned a deaf ear to God?

_____

_____

How might the life of Gideon have been different? _____

_____

_____

There are no clear answers to these two questions. Instead, we see in Gideon an example of how God can deliver His people if they are only willing to accept His forgiveness and believe about themselves what He believes about them.

A college football coach realized after much trouble in his own life, both personally and professionally, that he was not doing God's will. Even though he was successful athletically, he realized he was a failure spiritually. He needed God's forgiveness and a new direction...a second chance. One night this coach prayed to God for forgiveness, and he was forgiven. His life changed. He left the glamour of the world's

success. He sought reconciliation with his family. He sought direction from God. Can you think of a coach who fits this description?

The forgiveness that coach Bill McCartney (former head football coach at the University of Colorado) experienced has led to thousands of men understanding and accepting God's forgiveness in their own lives.

When we experience God's forgiveness, He is then able to appeal to our willingness to be used as His vessel.

Can you recall a time, after confessing your sins and being forgiven, that God opened up a ministry opportunity for you? Record your response below.

_____

_____

_____

God is in the business of taking ordinary people to achieve extraordinary results. It all begins with forgiveness and knowing you have a second chance. Think about ways God has used you. They may not compare to what Gideon or coach McCartney experienced. They could be even greater!

In the following Scriptures you will find many of the benefits available to us when we are forgiven and experience a second chance. Read the following Scriptures on forgiveness: Psalms 32:1-2; 103:12; Isaiah 1:18; 55:7; Mark 11:25; Ephesians 1:6-7; 2 Corinthians 5:17; Colossians 3:13; Hebrews 8:12; 1 John 2:1. Write the Scripture reference in the space beside the appropriate word or phrase.

     Happiness _____

     Reason together _____

     Against someone else _____

     Forgiving one another _____

     Pardon_____

     Merciful_____

     Advocate_____

     East is from the west _____

     New creature_____

     Redemption_____

Embrace the idea that you have a clean slate for the day that lies ahead—that you are a new creation and that you are open to new possibilities and opportunities. Even as you are working for God all through the day, as a student or at work, remember that God has forgiven you.

And when fresh, exciting, positive, second-chance opportunities present themselves, grab hold of them with both hands and don't let go.

Because I am forgiven, today I will demonstrate my second chance by

_____

_____

_____

_____

_____

Steps to Discovering the Winning Edge
1. God is totally faithful, a keeper of His word.
2. Confession and forgiveness put us in a position to be used by God.
3. God is in the business of taking ordinary people
to achieve extraordinary results.
4. When we experience God's forgiveness, He is then able to appeal
to our willingness to be used as His vessel.

Back 2 U
Do you think Vicki has discovered the winning edge?
How could you help Vicki experience God's forgiveness?
Have you experienced a second chance in your life?

Day 4: Distractions That Hinder

Principle: God gives second chances to those who trust Him.

Stacy has just completed her first semester in college. Her folks had told her that if her grades were good, then she could hold an off-campus job. Earning all As and Bs, she met their requirement. Stacy's roommate has been working at a restaurant and has told her boss about Stacy. Stacy felt OK about her roommate but had heard conflicting reports about how the boss related to his employees. Because of this, tension exists between Stacy and her roommate, and she is not able to focus clearly on what to do.

Did you notice how a distraction came into Stacy's life? Today's session deals with various distractions which may come into our lives and hinder us from discovering the winning edge.

The Distraction of Debt

Many people seem to create giant distractions with financial debt. Debt occurs in most instances when we refuse to pay the price up front. We opt for credit--a pledge against our future ability to pay. One of the major problems many college students face is their indebtedness. This a major distraction which can prevent a person from experiencing a second chance.

Refusing to pay the price up front is a lot like refusing to own up to our sin--we eventually accumulate a debt that becomes a burden. Earlier in the week, we looked at how God provided a way to pay off our spiritual debt, sin. Let's take a moment to review. Fill in the blanks in the statements below:

1. Seeking and receiving God's _____ is the first step in starting over.
2. Once we experience God's forgiveness, then we need to _____ ourselves.
3. Only the Lord sees our full _____.
4. God is totally _____, a keeper of His Word.
5. _____ and forgiveness puts us in a position to be used by God.

(Answers: 1. forgiveness; 2. forgive; 3. potential; 4. faithful; 5. confession)

We can be distracted in our relationship with God if we seek fulfillment in self-worth by way of things we acquire rather than seeking God. Look at the verses to the right. In Luke 12:28-31, Jesus commands us not to worry—not to set our hearts on the things that God has already promised to provide. In the space below, write down two things that you are often tempted to worry about or "run after," such as more money or possessions.

A closer look at Scripture reveals that the Bible has much to say about the stewardship of our possessions. Consider these four biblical principles below. Read the accompanying Scriptures, then answer the questions that follow.

> "If then God so clothes the grass, which today is in the field and tomorrow is thrown into the oven, how much more will He clothe you, O you of little faith? And do not seek what you should eat or what you should drink, nor have an anxious mind. For all these things the nations of the world seek after, and your Father knows that you need these things. But seek the kingdom of God, and all these things shall be added to you."
> —Luke 12:28-31

1.The love of money, not money itself, is the root of all evil. *Read 1 Timothy 6:10-11*. Does your choice of career indicate you have been guilty of loving money? ❑ Yes   ❑ No   ❑ Maybe

2. The person with the most toys at the end does not always win. *Read Luke 12:15*. If people could evaluate the totality of all of your "stuff," what do you think they would say describes your life? _____
_____

3.Trusting in what you have acquired is not guaranteed success. *Read Proverbs 11:28*. Describe one way your possessions have brought you happiness and satisfaction. _____
_____

4. God ultimately meets all of your needs. *Read Philippians 4:19*. How has God demonstrated Himself to be all sufficient in your life? _____
_____

Wanted: "Job requires only summer work on beaches, surrounded by sunshine and people. Earn $15,000 on weekends." A lifeguard? No way. You are a professional beach volleyball player. Eric Boyles, pro volleyball player from 1989-1994, loved playing a game that could also support his family. "Before I trusted Christ," Eric shares, "I had goals and relationships that were wrongly based. No matter how hard I tried without God in my life, I was still miserable. I had too much pride. Once I let the Lord break me of my pride and my own goals, I could more clearly see His will for

me."[1] What did $15,000 on weekends buy Eric? Is money a distraction in your life? ❑ Yes ❑ No ❑ Sometimes

Relationships That Distract

Poor choices concerning who we associate with can distract or harm us as well. Some students seem to get themselves into one sticky situation after another, making deals with students they shouldn't go into business with, forging relationships they sense are unhealthy from the outset, accepting friendship from people they don't like, or agreeing to provide a service or a manufacturing product they don't use or can't fully endorse. Eventually, these messy dealings become giants in students' lives. Relationships can definitely be a major distraction as you seek to discover the winning edge in your life.

Choosing a relationship is an important choice. In many ways, you become who your friends are and what your friends advise you to be and do.

What qualities are most important to you in determining whether to invest in a relationship with a person? Check all that apply:

❑ caring   ❑ trustworthy
❑ good reputation   ❑ encourages me to be the person
❑ sense of humor   Christ created me to be
❑ loyal   ❑ other _____

The qualities of a person all point to one thing--character. How can we tell the true character of a person? Jesus had some good insight to share when it came to questions of character: "You will know them by their fruits. Do men gather grapes from thornbushes or figs from thistles? Even so, every good tree bears good fruit, but a bad tree bears bad fruit...By their fruits you will know them" (Matt. 7:16-20).

Now think about a coworker or even a friend. Evaluate him or her in light of these guiding principles:
- Take a look at the person's track record, the way he or she has treated people in the past.
- Give yourself time to get acquainted with the person.
- Talk about value issues with the person.
- Watch how the person treats others who are less fortunate.

The Distraction of Jealousy

There is also a third potential giant--jealousy. Saul provides one example of someone who allowed jealousy to affect a relationship.

Read 1 Samuel 16:14-23 and 1 Samuel 18.

Because of his sin, an unrepentant heart, and an unwillingness to obey God in all things, King Saul fell from favor with God. And so it was that David came to Saul's court and became not only his chief physician, but his armorbearer. We are told that Saul loved David greatly.

The day came, however, when Saul's love turned to jealous hatred. David defeated Goliath and also killed a hundred other Philistines in winning the hand of Saul's daughter, Michal. Saul saw his daughter in love with David, the people of the land praising David for his victories, and the enemies of Israel fearful of David. Saul saw his own son, Jonathan, become more loyal to David than to himself. Most of all, Saul recognized that the Spirit of the Lord was no longer with him but was with David. Jealousy grew in his heart. And Saul sought to murder David.

Describe a time when you have been affected by jealousy.

_____

_____

_____

Debt, poor relationship choices, and jealousy can cause us to stumble.
However, wise choices can be made concerning these three.

Are you in need of a fresh touch from God in one of these areas? In the space below, write out a short prayer to God asking Him to help you be a giant slayer with the distraction you struggle with most.

Steps to Discovering the Winning Edge
1. Understand that debt occurs when we refuse to pay the price up front.
2. Recognize we become who our friends are.
3. Realize that jealousy destroys relationships.

Back 2 U
What are some potential distractions being put before Stacy?
If you were Stacy, would you take the job? Why? Why not?
How can these three distractions help you discover the winning edge in your walk with God and other people?

[1]Sliepka, Dave. "Catching Up With... ." *Sports Spectrum*, November 1996, 30.

Day 5: Self-disciplined Steps

Principle: God gives second chances to those who trust Him.

> Benjamin learned at an early age to develop a personal quiet time with the Lord. His folks were proud to see him at night in the quietness of his room with his Bible open on his bed. Now in college, Benjamin still continues this discipline of reading God's Word and seeking God first. At first, many of his college friends did not understand why he did this.

Trusting God requires that we maintain a self-disciplined life. We are all aware of times when we lack discipline and fall short of God's ideal. Oftentimes we go against our values and make bad, unwise decisions. During these times we need to trust God. Remember, He forgives and provides second chances.

There are steps we can take to help us maintain a self-disciplined life. Consider three specific actions that will help you to become more self-disciplined.

Discipline One: Maintain Values Through What You Read

One of the best ways to maintain values you hold to be true is to *remind yourself of what you believe on a daily basis*. The book of values is the Bible, and especially the teachings of Jesus and the Book of Proverbs. Immerse yourself in what the Bible says we are to believe and do. For some, this may be a first-time commitment and for others this is a continuation of what you know to be true.

Read Psalm 119:9-11. How does one remain pure?
1. By living _____
2. By seeking God _____
3. By not straying _____
4. By hiding the word _____
5. By not sinning _____

The Word of God is our guidebook to life. To a football player, it's his play book. To a painter, it's his brush. To a pianist, it's her _____.
To a student, it's her_____. The Bible determines how we live and act. James 1:22 says, "Be doers of the word, and not hearers only, deceiving yourselves."

The test is tomorrow. For some students this means a whole night of cramming. For others, it's a time to study and review. Others don't care and do nothing. As you seek to place God's Word in your life and to

control your actions, what grade would you give yourself when it comes to "doing" the Word of God? Circle one grade.

A+   A-   B+   B-   C+   C-   D+   D-   F+   F-

Do you want to do better? Read on!

Discipline Two: Keep Priorities

Jesus taught if we place our first emphasis on the kingdom of the Lord and on how to live in right standing with God, all of our other priorities will fall into line. Right priorities are important to God. Read Matthew 6:33. In other words, if we stay in right relationship with God, we have a much better chance of staying in right relationship with other people. Jot down one way you feel you can maintain a right relationship with the Lord. _____

_____

_____

One way to stay in right relationship with God is by talking to Him on a regular basis. If we discuss every decision, problem, action, and potential solution with the Lord in advance of pursuing it, and ask for the Lord to give us wisdom, we make much better choices.

A second way to stay in right relationship with God is to ask Him for wisdom. Many decisions that students face are unclear. We run the risk of making a mistake in our studies, our relationships, and our moral behavior when we try to operate out of our own limited understanding. James 1:5 reads, "If any of you lacks wisdom, let him ask of God, who gives to all liberally and without reproach, and it will be given to him" (also read vv. 6-8).

Knowledge is what we acquire on our own. God can surely help us gain knowledge in certain areas, however, we must work hard at obtaining and retaining this knowledge. But only God can give us wisdom.

List two areas of your life in which you need to gain knowledge.
1._____
2._____

List two areas in which you need to ask for God's wisdom.
1._____
2._____

Developing spiritual self-discipline demands that we maintain our values as well as keep our priorities in line. That which is important to us, we find time to do. How important is maintaining God's values in your

life? On the next page is a line. Make a mark on the line reflecting where you feel you are right now in maintaining God's values in your life.

Values Check

Far from God	Growing in Relationship	Close	In Touch

Discipline Three: Stay Disciplined

All discipline is ultimately self-discipline. You have to want to live a disciplined life. Read Proverbs 1:3.

Self-discipline often depends on developing accountability relationships. Find friends and mentors with whom you can talk over your desire to live a disciplined life, and put yourself into a relationship with them so that you are accountable to them for the way you live.

Ask their advice. Weigh what they say against God's Word to be sure their advice is good. Talk to the Lord about what they say to you, and listen for that "nudge" in your spirit that compels you to accept or reject what they say. If you have questions or concerns, raise them. If you come to the conclusion that their advice to you is sound, ask them for their help and encouragement as you try to do what they have advised you to do. The writer of Proverbs also wrote, "The way of a fool is right in his own eyes, but he who heeds counsel is wise" (12:15).

Disciplined steps require daily diligence. For most of us, these don't happen overnight. Be aware, however, you can destroy years of disciplined behavior in a matter of minutes, hours, days, or weeks. The apostle Paul said we are always to be on alert for the enemy who comes to try to trip us up and tempt us so that we fall away from the disciplined way of life we know is right.

Write down the name of someone you know who lives a disciplined life.

In what ways are you like this person? How are you different?

What steps can you take to improve your life to be more disciplined?

Born in Winnipeg, Manitoba, Canada in 1958, Terry Fox lived a life of determination and discipline. In March of 1976, Terry was diagnosed with osteosarcoma, a relatively rare bone cancer. Three days later, his right leg was amputated above the knee.

In spite of his personal tragedy, Terry's positive attitude led him to the idea of a cross-Canada run, a Marathon of Hope, in which he would raise money for cancer research. He prepared for two and one half years and on April 12, 1980, he began his run. Four and one-half months and 3,339 miles later, Terry had raised more than $2 million for cancer research. After the run, that figure increased to nearly $25 million.

Terry died on June 28, 1981. He became a symbol of commitment and self-discipline for many people in Canada and around the world.[1]

Stick to your values, keep your priorities in line, and maintain a disciplined life, then you will become a self-disciplined follower of Christ. Someone once said, "The race is not always to the swift, but to those who keep running."

The steps is I need to take today toward the disciplined life include _____
_____
_____
_____
_____

Steps to Discovering the Winning Edge
1. Trusting God requires that we maintain a self-disciplined life.
2. The Word of God is our guidebook to life.
3. Developing self-discipline demands that we maintain our values,
keep our priorities in line, and stay disciplined.

Back 2 U
How important are Benjamin's actions?
Do you think Benjamin is discovering the winning edge? Why?

[1]Johnson, Ann Donegan. *The Value of Facing a Challenge* (La Jolla, California: Value Communications, 1983), 63.

Facing Life's Fears

Day 1: Analyzing Anxiety

Principle: Facing life's fears produces positive actions.

Verse to Memorize This Week: "The Lord is my light and my salvation; whom shall I fear? The Lord is the strength of my life; of whom shall I be afraid?"--Psalm 27:1

> Annie struggled with taking tests. It wasn't that she was unprepared, because her grades were always among the top in her class. Getting there was the problem. Annie always studied her notes over and over again until she knew the material frontwards and backwards. However, when the professor passed out the tests, she became cold and clammy. Her mind was saying, "you're going to blow it." Her anxiety before taking the test would almost erase everything she had studied (at least she thought). After a few moments of breathing slowly and deeply, Annie would dive into the test.

What words would you use to describe "anxiety"? Hidden in the puzzle are 20 words associated with the feeling of anxiety. Circle the ones that you can find (look from left to right, right to left, up to down, down to up, and diagonally). These words are listed at the end of this session. Give it a good shot before taking a look!

```
A K R E J E D S S E R T S H I P
T R T A G I T A T I O N K T A R
E R U N F A I L U R E A G S N E
N E R V O U S L T D E R I T X S
S S M N R O T F N W O R R Y I S
E A O D A E R D I S P A I R E U
A D I S C O U R A G E M E N T R
K H L U R P H S F F N I A P Y E
```

45

Anxiety, despair, and discouragement cripple and leave us ineffective in the kingdom of God. Fight the giants in your life now...in strength. Or fight the giants later...in weakness.

Few of us are ever able to enter a conflict and emerge victorious without getting anxious in some way. The anxiety may not be severe, or even visible for that matter, but being anxious is nearly always a part of winning.

When you face a giant, you have two choices: You can fight and expect to win or run away, only to face another giant. In running from a giant, you are only delaying the showdown. You can face your giant today, with anxiousness to take whatever wounds you receive, and go forward with victory and scars. Or you can run from the giant, become discouraged and faint in your heart, and then face a giant later on in a weakened state. The more you allow anxiety to cause you to run from giants, the weaker you become.

How does God's Word address the issue of anxiety in my life? Take a look at 1 Peter 5:6-7. Then answer the following questions to the best of your ability based on what you read in the Scripture passage.

What do you think is meant by the word _____
_____
How can you humble yourself before God? _____
_____
How can you "cast" your anxiety on God? _____
_____
_____

Anxiety can come by way of many life experiences. What may be the cause of anxiety in your life may not even be noticed by someone else. Also, what may cause you anxiety today may not even be an issue for you tomorrow.

Can you identify some of the causes of your anxiety lately? List five causes below:

_____
_____
_____
_____
_____
_____
_____
_____
_____
_____

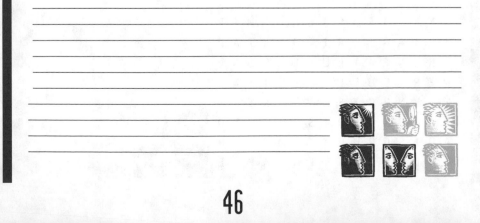

God is interested in every source of anxiety you are facing, both large and small. He desires for us to take these to Him in prayer. Choose one cause of anxiety from your list, and write a prayer to God asking for His help.

Jeff Kemp, son of the former vice-presidential candidate, Jack Kemp, played for 11 years in the National Football League. Jeff experienced many lessons from the ups and downs of his career. He began as a fifth-string quarterback in the Los Angeles Rams' camp in 1981. He moved to third string, then to fourth, third, second, first, second, first, second, third, second, and then to the first string.

"That's the crucible of my career––that I had to make the team every year," Jeff says. "It drove me to Christ. Soon I realized that God was using this experience of football to develop my faith, to cause me to depend upon Him. I saw all of football as tied to my spiritual life. Had I had complete success, I wouldn't have grown as close to God as I have, and my pride would have taken more of a hold on my life."[1]

Some students wake up in the morning nervous about the day ahead. They go to bed at night, even after saying their prayers, and toss and turn as they think about what lies ahead, and even worse, what *might* lie ahead. Other students have anxiety attacks on a regular basis, with palpitations of the heart, shortness of breath, and cold sweats. Others live in a state in which constant worry and dread lie under the surface of all their other emotions. If they aren't worried about something, they think up something to worry about, because joy and peace of heart are uncomfortable states for them. Does this describe you or a friend?

Remember these three encouraging guidelines as you confront anxiety:
1. **Remind yourself who you are.** The God who created you loves you and knows what's best for you. You are special in His sight, a person of value.
2. **Recognize your dependency on God.** Life's greatest lesson is to find your strength in God. In order for us to win over life's battles, we need to depend on Him for everything.
3. **Realize a life outside yourself.** Anxiety can cause us to turn inward and cause us to have a "pity party." Get up and do something for someone else.

On a scale of 1-10, with one being the highest and 10 the lowest, how would you rank yourself in terms of living by these guidelines? _____

Which step is the most difficult for you to live by? Why?

Spend some time in prayer asking God to help you incorporate these three guidelines into your life.

Write your Scripture memory verse for this chapter in the space below and review your verses from other chapters. _____

_____
_____
_____
_____
_____
_____

Steps to Discovering the Winning Edge
1. Anxiety can come by way of many life experiences.
2. God is interested in every one of our concerns and problems, both large and small.
3. Face anxiety by reminding yourself who you are, recognizing your dependency on God, and realizing a life outside yourself.

Back 2 U
In what way can you identify with Annie in the case study?
How do you think Annie can solve her problem with anxiety?
How can anxiety keep you from discovering the winning edge?

(Puzzle words: anxiety, discouragement, weak, fear, faint, worry, nervous, turmoil, agitation, failure, hurt, dread, sad, tired, torn, run, stress, pain, pressure, and tense) It's always great to find the answers!

[1]Victor, Lee. "Snatching Victory From Defeat." *Sports Spectrum*, November 1996, 5.

Day 2: Promises of Provision
Principle: Facing life's fears produces positive action.

> Monique worked between 10-15 hours a week in the school cafeteria. Jobs were hard to come by, but this job fulfilled a requirement for her special student loan. Coming from a poor family, Monique worked hard to provide for herself. She even made sacrifices in order to send a few dollars home to her folks every month. She was committed to working and studying hard, as well as to being faithful in her tithing to her church. She knew God would remain faithful in meeting her needs.

Is there something that the Lord has compelled you, commanded you, or convicted you to do that you have not been courageous enough or faithful to carry out--possibly on campus or with a friend?   ❑ Yes   ❑ No
If you answered yes, then describe your response in the space below.

Recognize that God's Word is filled with commandments and promises. Take them personally, recognizing that they apply to you. God provides what we need in order to do what He asked. The Scripture passages below contain promises from God. Under the heading, "What did God promise?" write down what you believe is promised in each reference.

Scripture reference	What did God promise?
Galatians 3:26-29	
Ezekiel 36:26-27	
John 14:14	
James 4:7-8	
Philippians 4:7	

Remind yourself that the Lord promised to take care of you. However, His promises hinge on your obedience to Him. Ask Him to make His presence real to you now, to give you both the courage and the comfort to take the action that you need to take.

God Provides a Way to Live Victoriously Above Life's Challenges

Think back to Moses for a moment. Moses spent 40 years on the back side of the wilderness because he killed an Egyptian who brutally mistreated one of his fellow Hebrews. Moses knew that Pharaoh would search for him to kill him. Pharaoh became a giant in Moses' life. And Moses ran from him.

But Moses did not rid Pharaoh from his life until he confronted him in the power of the Lord. Moses faced other giants in the interim, but his first giant never went away. It was to Pharaoh that the Lord sent Moses with a message: "Let my people go." As much as he didn't want to go, Moses had to return to Egypt and square off against Pharaoh for his own purpose to be fulfilled in the Lord and for God's people to be delivered.

Moses faced Pharaoh not just one time but many times. Each time Moses made the same request: "Let us go to worship the Lord." Each time the answer from Pharaoh was the same: "No."

In the course of confronting Pharaoh, Moses was wounded and scarred. His own people began to blame him for the extra persecution that they received. Confronting the giant of Pharaoh wasn't easy for Moses.

The Lord, however, honored Moses' obedience and courage in facing Pharaoh. He stepped in and caused such overwhelming devastation to Pharaoh and the families of the Egyptians that Pharaoh relented and let the Hebrew people leave Egypt––but only temporarily. After several days, Pharaoh sent his chariots and soldiers in hot pursuit of Moses and the children of Israel.

As the children of Israel found the Red Sea before them and the army of Pharaoh behind them, they became afraid. They cried out, "Because there are no graves in Egypt, have you taken us away to die in the wilderness?...It would have been better for us to serve the Egyptians than that we should die in the wilderness." Have you ever been in a situation where you felt this way?
❏ Yes   ❏ No

Moses responded to the people with giant-slaying wisdom. He said, "Do not be afraid. Stand still, and see the salvation of the Lord, which He will accomplish for you today. For the Egyptians whom you see today, you shall see no more forever. The Lord will fight for you, and you shall hold your peace" (see Ex. 14:10-24).

Moses had personally faced down the giant of Pharaoh. Moses knew that this giant was vulnerable, that God was on his side, that God had delivered the people from the death angel at the time of the Passover, and that God was bigger than Pharaoh.

Look closely at this week's Scripture memory verse: "The Lord is my light and my salvation; whom shall I fear? The Lord is the strength of my life; of whom shall I be afraid?" (Ps. 27:1).

List several ways the following truths from Scripture have proven trustworthy in your own life:
"The Lord is my light"

"The Lord is my stronghold"

Thomas O. Chisholm and William M. Runyan are probably not household names. They teamed together, Chisholm with words and Runyan with music, to write a great hymn of how God provides for our needs. Read the words to "Great Is Thy Faithfulness." As you read, think of your own needs right now as a student.

> "Great Is Thy Faithfulness"
> Great is Thy faithfulness, O God, my Father,
> There is no shadow of turning with Thee;
> Thou changest not, Thy compassions, they fail not;
> As Thou has been, Thou forever wilt be. (Chorus)
>
> Summer and winter, and springtime and harvest,
> Sun, moon, and stars in their courses above
> Join with all nature in manifold witness
> To Thy great faithfulness, mercy, and love. (Chorus)
>
> Pardon for sin and a peace that endureth,
> Thine own dear presence to cheer and to guide;
> Strength for today and bright hope for tomorrow,
> Blessings all mine, with ten thousand beside! (Chorus)
>
> (Chorus): Great is Thy faithfulness! Great is Thy faithfulness!
> Morning by morning new mercies I see;
> All I have needed, Thy hand hath provided;
> Great is Thy faithfulness, Lord unto me![1]

Go back and underline or circle the most meaningful words or statements in the lyrics of the hymn. Although the hymn is quite old, the message is as contemporary as needs you express to God.

Describe some ways has God shown His faithfulness to you.

_____

_____

God's Provision

Turn to Genesis 32. In this Scripture passage, Jacob provides us with three prayer principles. We are wise to do what Jacob did, to cast ourselves totally and completely on the Lord and apply the following:

• *First Prayer Principle:* When you face a giant, you are wise to recount how the Lord has provided for you in the past (see vv. 9-10).

• *Second Prayer Principle:* Don't be afraid to admit your weaknesses or feelings to the Lord (see v. 11).

• *Third Prayer Principle*: Put your sights on your future, not on your past or present (see v. 12).

Jacob discovered that God made provision for him as he prayed. Have you felt the same type of provision in your prayer life? How? _____

_____

We have all been frightened to the point that we have prayed for protection. What did Jacob do when he feared an attack from his brother, Esau? Read verses 10-11 again. What two characteristics of his prayer did Jacob show?

_____

Evaluate your own prayer life. The last time you prayed, did you do so in a spirit of humility? Gratitude?

Did you claim God's provision for your life? ❑ Yes   ❑ No

Review this week's Scripture memory verse as well as the memory verses from the previous chapters.

Steps to Discovering the Winning Edge

1. When you face a giant, you are wise to recount how the Lord has provided for you in the past.
2. Don't be afraid to admit your weaknesses or feelings to the Lord.
3. Put your sights on your future--not the past or present.

Back 2 U

Would you call Monique a typical student?
What impresses you about Monique's life?
Is she close to discovering the winning edge?

Day 3: Attitudes that Win

Principle: Facing life's fears produces positive actions.

Jerry was accused of taking "happy pills." The moment his feet touched the floor until he laid his head on his pillow at night, Jerry's outlook was upbeat. His fraternity buddies enjoyed his company, and he was often voted on to lead various functions. Everyone knew that Jerry gave his very best. It was apparent that Jerry had the right attitude to succeed in life. This was a choice he chose to make.

Attitudes

Attitudes are the invisible heartbeats of our minds. Just as the heart sends our blood to nourish and cleanse every part of our bodies so that we can function at our maximum potential, so our attitudes cause our minds to take in certain information, reject other information, and cause us to function mentally in ways that bring us success.

Attitudes are more important than fears. They are controlling values for our behavior. Over time, our attitudes become so deeply embossed on our minds that they are like mental and emotional habits. We think in certain ways because we have chosen to view life in a certain way over time.

We become not only what we think but how we think about what we think. Attitude is a value and a positive or negative charge that we add to opinion. Attitudes have both direction and strength.

A positive attitude attracts positive ideas and positive opinions. A negative attitude attracts negative ideas and negative opinions. Attitudes also produce behavior of like kind. Positive attitudes result in positive behavior. The stronger the attitude, the more likely the behavior. In other words, the more positive your attitude, the more positive your behavior.

We need a strong positive attitude to survive and conquer in today's world. The stronger the heartbeat, the stronger the body. The stronger the positive attitude, the greater the motivation toward success in facing giants.

Examine the verses below. In the space that follows, summarize what each Scripture passage has to say about positive attitudes.

Psalm 118:24 _____

_____

_____

Lamentations 3:21-24 _____

_____

Proverbs 4:23 _____

_____

We make choices every day, from when to get up, what to wear, what to do--all the way to bedtime. We choose whether to face each day with a positive or negative attitude. A positive attitude really does make a difference!

Four components of a positive attitude
Face Today's Giant Today
Many of us put off slaying some of the giants in our lives in hopes that they will go away, or that we will somehow grow in our ability to slay a particular giant at a future time. Today's giants need to be faced today and defeated today. Giants that are left alone prevent us from discovering the winning edge.

Identify a bad habit in your life. You don't have to write it down. Simply identify it in your mind. Now, identify a good habit in your life. Which one makes you feel better? Which one do you want to keep?

On the scale below, indicate with a mark where you are in developing attitudes that win.

Negative attitudes   **Positive Attitudes**

_____

Choose To Be A Nice Person
Ask a person what the most important things in life are, and you are going to find intangibles: love, joy, peace, faith, hope. Although many of us spend a great deal of time pursuing tangibles--jobs, houses, cars, gadgets, good grades, and being well liked on campus--it is the intangibles that we can't do without. These contribute to one being a nice person to be around. It's your choice. You can be the most athletic person on campus, the prettiest cheerleader--and not be liked at all. Or you can choose to be a nice person.

List three specific actions you can take in choosing to be a nice person.
1._____
2._____
3._____

_____

Do Your Best Everyday
Our attitudes aren't fixed, they can change from day to day. We should begin each day by saying to ourselves, **"I am going to have the very best attitude I can have today. I am going to give my best to the tasks that lie before me."**

54

On the lines below, write down three things you are facing in the next few days or weeks that require a positive attitude. Then pray and ask God to help you begin each day with the statement that was suggested at the bottom of the previous page.

1. _____

2. _____

3. _____

Dwight Moody told a story about an incident that happened shortly after he started preaching. He had preached the best sermon that he knew to preach, and a number of people had been blessed by it. After the service, however, a local English teacher came up to him and said, "You had a nice sermon, but you made 26 grammatical errors."

Moody was dumbstruck for a few moments, not knowing how to respond. Finally, he felt as if the Lord had dropped these words into his mouth, "Well, ma'am, I'm doing the best I can with what I've got, are you?"

How would you critique what you have accomplished today? Check your response.

_____	A waste of time
_____	So-so
_____	Stuck in neutral
_____	Pretty good, if I say so myself
_____	Hard to get any better

Be Thankful

It is possible for you to be grateful for the good things that come your way. Call to your remembrance the good times in the past and express your thankfulness to God for His provision to you, His deliverance of you, and the gracious gifts and blessings He has given you. Especially as a student, God is still loving and providing for you.

In 1620, about 100 men and women came to America and created a settlement called Plymouth. Their first winter was an incredibly bitter one. Death took a heavy toll. By the end of the first year, more of their number were in the cemetery than were gathered around the common dinner tables. Food was running very low. Governor Bradford began issuing just five grains of corn to each person for a day's ration. For more than a month, each person in Plymouth had only five grains of corn to eat a day!

The fortunes of the settlers changed with the spring weather and the peace they forged with the Native Americans. For many years Governor Bradford took the opportunity at their annual Thanksgiving meal to remind the settlers of God's faithfulness in providing

for them in the past by placing five grains of corn beside each plate. When was the last time you sat down and counted your blessings, naming them one by one? Use the lines below to write a note of thankfulness for the blessings in your life.I am thankful, God, for _____

_____

_____

Psalm 118:24 reads, "This is the day the Lord has made; we will rejoice and be glad in it." Every new day is God's gift to us. He makes each day for us. What then is our proper response? Just from looking at the Scripture above, fill in the blanks to the following:

Our response is to _____and be _____ : _____ ____ .

Caution: Danger Ahead!

Proverbs 4:23 advises, "Keep your heart with all diligence, for out of it spring the issues of life." Do you watch what you think? Do you watch how you feel about things? This is what the writer means when he writes, "guard your heart."

Thoughts ➤ Words ➤ Actions ➤ Habits ➤ Character ➤ Destiny

- Watch your thoughts; they become words.
- Watch your words; they become actions.
- Watch your actions; they become habits.
- Watch your habits; they become your character.
- Watch your character; it becomes your destiny.

Your attitudes are your invisible heartbeat, the very wellspring of your entire life--for good or bad, for success or failure.

Steps to Discovering the Winning Edge
1. Face today's giant today.
2. Choose to be a nice person.
3. Do your best everyday.
4. Be thankful.

Back 2 U
How will you allow your thoughts to guide your life? Does Jerry in the case study have the right attitude to succeed in life? How can you be more positive with yourself and others?

Day 4: Face to Face with Fear

Principle: Facing life's fears produces positive actions.

Trey had one of the leading parts in the spring drama production. He had performed in a few plays in high school, but nothing to the extent of what he was soon going to do on campus. The night before the play was to open, Trey's mind raced with doubts. "What if I forget my lines?" "What if I get a sore throat?" "What if some of my friends see me mess up?" He needed to talk to someone about his fears but was afraid to share them with others in the production. Fear was beginning to paralyze Trey's confidence.

Name That Fear!

Let's take a look at some of the "fears" which plague mankind. Below you find a listing of many of our fears. How many can you identify as you "Name That Fear"? Match each fear with its correct definition. Don't be afraid if you can answer only a few. All is in fun...

Fear of spiders	acrophobia
Fear of crowds	agoraphobia
Fear of closed places	pyrophobia
Fear of fear	xenophobia
Fear of strangers	arachnophobia
Fear of heights	phophobia
Fear of blushing	claustrophobia
Fear of crossing the street	dromophobia
Fear of water	erythrophobia
Fear of open spaces	hydrophobia
Fear of fire	zoophobia
Fear of dirt	mysophobia
Fear of animals	pathophobia
Fear of the number 13	ochlophobia
Fear of the disease	triskaidekaphobia

Understand Fear

At times, fear manifests itself as fear of failure. It may come in the form of fear of embarrassment in front of a student group or fear of loss. The most debilitating thing about this type of fear is that it prevents us from reaching out for what we might be able to achieve. *This type of fear paralyzes.* Fear compels us to think, "If I don't do this, I'll stay alive, and everything will be all right." Unfortunately, fear disables to the point that we may be alive, but rarely is everything all right. He who is paralyzed into doing nothing quickly stagnates and takes no risk. Such a person doesn't grow. Life without growth and risk is not much of a life!

Circle the appropriate answer following each statement:
- Fear prevents people from reaching out for that which they might be able to achieve.　❑ True　　❑ False
- Fear can be paralyzing.　❑ True　　　❑ False
- The person who is paralyzed by fear frequently is a risk taker.
❑ True　　　❑ False
- You can live with fear and still grow.　❑ True　　❑ False

Read Matthew 8:23-27. List a "fear" that is exhibited in this passage.

Fear is reactive; it is rooted in our emotions, and it excites our emotions. Once fear has taken hold, we are rarely capable of focusing our thinking. Logic, reasoning, and evidence all tend to fold in the face of fear.

Many coaches and players have known the stinging pain of losing a game primarily because the home team was more scared of the opponent or the opponent was scared of the home team. Teams really do well if they play scared. Rather, they do well if they play "scarier"—believing themselves to be the meanest, biggest, toughest, smartest, quickest, and best team on the field. If you've played in a competitive sport, you know this is true.

Fear is rarely focused, which is part of its nature. Fear is rooted in "I don't know" and "I don't understand" far more than in "I know" or "I believe."

Understand Confidence
Faith is best placed in God, not oneself. He is the One who knows all, can do all, and is never too late or too early. He alone has all wisdom and knowledge and resources. Within that broader context of faith, however, a person can feel confident. Paul perhaps has said it best: "I can do all things through Christ who strengthens me" (Phil. 4:13).

Self-confidence lies primarily in knowing the following three things about yourself as you ponder a particular decision or take up a challenge.
- Have you prepared?
- Have you anticipated the outcome of your actions?
- Have you believed in something that gives you strength?

When we have prepared ourselves, anticipated the outcomes, and believed in something, we are many steps ahead of most people when it comes to having the confidence it takes to discover the winning edge.

Fear and self-doubt are paralyzing. Faith and self-confidence are mobilizing. The only way to break out of a cycle of fear is to take action. Do something as

an expression of your faith in God and faith in your preparation and enthusiasm. Act on the opportunities that present themselves.

The coin of confidence always has two sides—faith and fear.

Of course, not all opportunities are worth taking. That's where your preparation will help sift out good opportunities from not-so-good ones. Trust your abilities, rooted in your faith that God will help you discern and make wise choices as you ask questions, weigh options, and look for hidden dangers. In the end, if you firmly believe you are looking at a risk worth taking and a challenge worth pursing, go for it!

Wishing and hoping don't make things happen. Preparing, committing, and then taking action are the keys to moving forward. Action brings one face to face with fear. Fear that is allowed to run wild, go unchecked, and remain unbridled turns into panic. Panic is the feeling of being out of control.

The following is a paraphrase of Matthew 8:23-27 which you read earlier: Jesus boarded a small, simple fishing boat. The disciples followed Him. It was a calm day on the Sea of Galilee. Suddenly a storm appeared. It caught the disciples by surprise. Jesus was asleep. The disciples were afraid. By saying, "us" and "we" (v. 25), they admitted that they felt even Jesus was in trouble!

Jesus quietly rebuked them. Notice that in the middle of the storm Jesus was in perfect peace. He wasn't mad, but perhaps disappointed, in their lack of faith. He then rebuked the winds and the waves, and they became calm again. This was a miracle. He truly is Lord of all.

Recall the last time you were paralyzed with fear. In the space below, write down some of the things you missed out on due to holding back because of fear. In other words, what were some of the consequences of your choosing to listen to fear instead of acting in confidence? _____

_____

The Scriptures assures us as children of God that God will take care of us. He is our source of strength. He is right beside us during any storm. He overcomes any fear. He models for us His peace even in fearful situations.

Which would you rather have controlling your life—fear or faith? Why? _____

_____

_____

On a separate sheet of paper, write out a prayer to God asking Him to help you overcome the fears in your life. Make a commitment to share your decision to eliminate

paralyzing fear from your life with a friend.

Wang Weilin had known the feeling of fear before in his life. He was not different than any of us. What was he thinking when as a young student he stood before a group of army tanks advancing on Tiananmen Square on June 5, 1989? Had he become insane? Was he looking to become a martyr? The picture showed this young Chinese man standing courageously before a certain death. The tanks stopped. He was a young man driven with purpose.

Healthy Fear Leads to Life
There is a degree of fear that is healthy. This fear has been built into us by our Creator so we might preserve our lives and fulfill His purpose for our lives. This fear causes us to keep our children from wandering into streets. It compels us to keep laws, including God's divine laws. This kind of fear leads to life.

Look up the Scripture references below. In the space that is provided, list the benefits or rewards of having a healthy fear (respect, honor) of the Lord.

Scripture reference	Benefits
Psalm 19:9	
Psalm 111:10	
Proverbs 1:7	
Proverbs 8:13	
Proverbs 9:10	
Proverbs 10:27	
Proverbs 19:23	

Fear makes us vulnerable when we become detached from the source of true self-confidence, the Lord Himself. Pray for the courage to stand face to face with life's fears, keeping your eyes fixed on Jesus, our Source of peace.

Today, to face my fears, I will _____

_____

Steps to Discovering the Winning Edge
1. Faith is best placed in God, not oneself.
2. Fear and self-doubt are paralyzing.
3. Faith and self-confidence are mobilizing.

Back 2 U
Think of a time when fear paralyzed you, how did you respond?
What advice would you give Trey to help him with his confidence?
Is your lifestyle is one of fear or confidence?

Day 5: Defeating the Partners of Fear

Principle: Facing life's fears produces positive actions.

> Alex was determined that it wouldn't happen again. He thought he had learned his lesson last semester. But now he was facing writing another major English paper the night before it was due. How could he let it slip up on him again? It surely wasn't any fun for him last time...and it wouldn't be any easier now. Where did the time go?

Have you ever seen a train? Most of us have. Have you noticed that the train is almost always led by a locomotive engine. Imagine if you will, that the locomotive is fear. The locomotive is usually pulling behind it 10 to 50 to 100 cars. On our train of fear, the locomotive is pulling five freight cars. Each car carries a different partner of fear. The first car is carrying procrastination. The second, overwork. The third, time wasters. The fourth, confusion. And the fifth car is carrying perfectionism! Guess where the train is headed? Imagine each boxcar is depositing it's contents in your life.

Procrastination—Car #1
Procrastination--putting off until tomorrow what should be done today--is often a manifestation of fear. We stall because we are afraid of taking action. What are we afraid of?

Sometimes we fear doing the wrong thing or making the wrong choice. Other times we fear that there may be no need for us in the future if we finish a current job. Sometimes we fear that we won't able to finish a job.If you are a habitual procrastinator, ask yourself, why am I afraid to finish a job?

Below are some suggestions to make sure procrastination isn't a controlling force in your life. Look at each suggestion. Put a ✔ beside the two statements that you feel are a part of your life and you are comfortable with. Then put an ✘ next to the two which give you the most trouble.
- ❑ Admit that you are a procrastinator.
- ❑ Have the desire to stop procrastinating.
- ❑ Believe that you can, with God's help, break the habit.
- ❑ Resolve to get into the habit of action.
- ❑ Accomplish tasks daily that will permit you to exercise success.
- ❑ Think of the good feelings you have when you experience success.
- ❑ Associate with more action-oriented people.

The car of procrastination can be left in your life long after the locomotive has disappeared! However, it doesn't have to be that way!

Overwork—Car #2

Work is healthy. But for some students, work can be an obsession. You push yourself to do and do and do. You never "turn off" at the end of the day. What's behind overwork? Very often it is a fear of not living up to another person's expectations or a fear that if one says no to a particular task or project, you will be ridiculed, lose face, or never be given the opportunity to be involved in the ministry of the church again.

A pattern of overwork is often driven by a lack of faith in God to provide what we need. "Workaholics" truly are addicted to work. They can't imagine life that isn't framed by deadlines and "to do" lists. If you fall into that category, schedule some downtime for yourself. If you must put it on a schedule, do so. Give yourself at least two or three hours a week in which you refuse to schedule anything. Use that time for spontaneous activity, rest, and recreation.

If you had three hours to "enjoy" for the sheer purpose of enjoyment, what would you do? Jot down a couple ways you could spend those three hours.

_____

_____

Paul wrote the Corinthians, "Let all things be done decently and in order" (1 Cor. 14:40).

Don't be afraid to trust God to supply your needs. In saying no to over-obligation of your time and energy, you may actually be saying yes to Him, giving God room and time to speak to you, lead you, and guide you in ways that will make you even more effective and efficient.

Car # 2 is rounding the bend and headed straight for you. What are you going to do?

Time Wasters—Car #3

When we waste time on trivial, unimportant activities, we often face deadlines and obligations somewhat unexpectedly––to the point that we are fearful that we will not be able to succeed. Somehow, we know we have wasted our time.

What are some of your time wasters? The list below is not all inclusive. However, it does represent some of the things in our lives which can demand time. Put an ✗ beside those which you do a lot and a ✔ beside those which don't bother you much.

For a college student, life has lots of time wasters. Among them are:

- ❑ unimportant phone calls
- ❑ goofing off with friends
- ❑ long lines
- ❑ procrastination

❑ traffic jams   ❑ most television programs
❑ doing laundry   ❑ daydreaming

At the end of a day engaged in such activities--even if there is a certain amount of enjoyment in some of them--a student is likely to feel panic that he hasn't done anything that truly needed to be done. At the end of a college career engaged in such activities, a student is likely to feel a deep-seated fear that she might not graduate on time.

This car won't make a major stop in your life when you learn how to manage your time.

Confusion—Car #4

Confusion is nearly always associated with fear. It's definitely one of the cars on the train. Satan would love to make a stop in your life and leave this car. And wherever a spirit of confusion reigns, we know that evil is afoot. Paul wrote to Timothy, "God has not given us a spirit of fear, but of power and of love and of a sound mind" (2 Tim. 1:7). A sound mind is free of confusion.

In a confusing situation, ask the Lord for clarity. Get to the root of what is causing the constant state of upheaval or disorientation in your life. Perhaps it simply exists because you enrolled in too many classes for this term. Eliminate the source of confusion or develop clarity and control the scene.

After discerning the root cause of the confusion around you, ask the Holy Spirit to impart peace to your heart and a sense of order to your mind. First Corinthians 14:33 asserts, "God is not the author of confusion but of peace."

Take a moment now to stop...Ask God for a mind focused on clarity and not confusion. Ask God for discernment. Ask God to give you peace in your heart. After doing so, write some actions you can take to affirm God's presence.

God wants to remove the element of confusion from your life.

Perfectionism—Car #5

Finally, fear is linked closely to perfectionism. Perfectionism is a desire to do everything in an A+ fashion, without any error. It is rooted in a personal fear of failure--including a fear that we won't be loved, included, appreciated, or valued if we make mistakes or fail to live up to the highest standard.

Paul wrote to the Romans, "All have sinned and fall short of the glory of God" (Rom. 3:23).

It is not possible for any of us to be perfect. Even so, many people try to be perfect, only to live in constant fear of being less than perfect.

Perfectionism is nearly always self-imposed. The perfectionist has the task of recognizing that his perfectionism is a giant that will keep him from completing many things. If you are continually striving to get something perfect, you are not likely to let it go, trust God with it, and move on to the next challenge He has for you. As a result, you can miss doing much of what the Lord wants you to do.

Take a look at Matthew 14:22-33. Why were the disciples confused when they saw Jesus walking on the water? _____

_____

Jesus was trying to teach His disciples that instead of allowing the partners of fear to control them, they should trust Him. Did you notice that before He calmed the wind, Jesus asked the disciples why they doubted? The powerful lesson is that Jesus may give us an answer with His presence right in the middle of that which we are fearing. In other words, before He removes our fear, He wants us to know that He is with us and we can depend on Him.

Also notice that the climax of the story is not the calming of the wind but rather the worship of the Savior (see v. 33). Only our Lord is worthy of our worship. He alone can dispel our fears.

List the five boxcars (partners of fear).

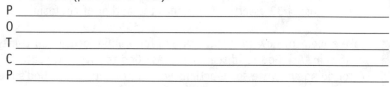

P _____
O _____
T _____
C _____
P _____

Steps to Discovering the Winning Edge
1. Understanding that the partners of fear include procrastination, overwork, time wasters, confusion, and perfectionism is the first step in dealing with fear.
2. In identifying the partners of fear, you take a big step toward conquering them.
3. Trust in the Lord to help you conquer your fears.

Back 2 U
Which "partner" concerns you most as a student? Ask God to give you clarity and focus to avoid the partners of fear.

Focusing on the Basics

Day 1: Family of One–the Basic Family

Principle: Committed faith focuses on the basics.

Verse to Memorize This Week: "Therefore, whatever you want men to do to you, do also to them, for this is the Law and the Prophets."--Matthew 7:12

> Meredith was seen by her close friends in college as a very lucky young woman. The fact is that Meredith felt luck had nothing to do with her situation. She was raised in a Christian home, surrounded by godly parents and grandparents. Now she is starting her own life in the dorm at school. She is in a suite with three other females. They all seem friendly. Although she shares her room with one of the other young women, Meredith has her own space and has begun her family of one.

Think about this statement and how it can be applied to your life: "Family of one!" As a student, do you feel you are a family of one?
❏ Yes   ❏ No   ❏ Maybe
Explain. _____
_____

Even though you have a biological family, as a student you realize you are now "adopting" another family. This family will be made up of mostly other students and faculty on campus.

Each new member of your family will play a significant role in the development of your character. Describe in a word or two how you feel the following will affect your life:
Roommate _____
Closest friend on campus _____
Favorite professor _____
Family at home _____

Bernie Carbo played for 12 years as a major league baseball player. He was drafted by

Cincinnati out of high school and was voted "Rookie of the Year" in 1970. At the age of 23, he played in the 1970 World Series along with Johnny Bench, Pete Rose, and Tony Perez. During the 1975 World Series, and as a player for the Red Sox, he batted .429. He was a hero in the fans' eyes.

However, his personal life was a struggle. Carbo had suffered from a sexual attack as a child which affected relationships later in life. He became an addict to "performance-enhancing" drugs. He was miserable. Carbo retired in 1980. Life got no easier. Both parents died within a short period of each other, leaving many unspoken, unresolved feelings. His drug addiction was still an issue. He also struggled with attention deficit disorder.

On December 26, 1992, Carbo contemplated suicide. But instead of killing himself, he contacted a former teammate who along with another former teammate, took him to a psychiatric hospital for help. It was there that his roommate, a retired preacher, shared Jesus with Carbo. Later, a nurse shared the Bible and prayed with Carbo. He gave his life to Christ and began "The Diamond Club," reaching out to children through baseball clinics and camps.

His message is simple and clear. His spoken and lived-out priorities are now heard and seen as:
- Read the Bible
- Pray
- Keep Satan Away
- Tell Others About Jesus[1]

Notice what happened to Carbo in his family of one. He faced countless successes and setbacks. Ultimately his life was a shambles. Who would you say contributed to the outcome in his life? "He contacted a former roommate who along with another former teammate..." Even though he was a family of one and facing failure, there were others who were a significant part of his "adopted" family. Thankfully, he knew he could count on them to help him. In his roommate, Carbo saw love and care—basics of rebuilding a meaningful family of one. In their actions he saw someone he could imitate. Carbo's life has now impacted a new "extended family." But first he had to get his house in order. What does your family of one look like today?

Read Ephesians 5:1-2. This passage speaks of walking in "_____, as _____ also has loved us and _____ _____for us, an _____ and a _____ to God for a sweet-smelling aroma."

Developing the basics of a family of one depends on many factors. Each demands time and effort to insure success. The end results are not always guaranteed. However, as we depend upon God to guide us, we

make every possible effort in becoming a Christ-honoring person.

Time, communication, daily disciplines, and a giving, caring atmosphere are necessary and important elements of a healthy life. If you ask people what the basics are for a good life, they will probably zero in on traits such as these:

1. Spend quality time together with your family.
Doing things together, including eating meals together and attending church together. The people who are important to you must share some of your time. You need to make sure time is allotted to each of these persons. How much time do you spend on building a healthy relationship with your roommate? How much quality time do you spend with your friends on campus?

No matter what your biological family was like (hopefully it was loving), what your family will be in the future depends on your character today. Quality time spent with family speaks of a positive character and healthy life.

2. Communicate with one another.
Talking over the day's activities and events, as well as campus news, dorm news, or news from back home is essential. Your new home life is marked by frequent and free-flowing communication.

Our levels of communication range from sharing only surface feelings such as when we first wake up in the morning and responding, "I'm doing fine. How are you doing?" to really sharing our true feelings in an argument or a debate.

Complete the following exercise. Think about something positive that Meredith could do in her suite to communicate with her suitemates. Write that action in the first space, then complete the rest of the responses.

For example, Meredith's roommate might say to her:
When you help me with my homework,
I feel appreciated,
And so I thank you for what you did,
Instead of griping about my being stupid and needing help.

Positive Feeling Response
When you _____,
I feel _____,
And so I _____,
Instead of _____.

3. Maintain standards related to discipline and responsibility for yourself and others.
Relational discipline includes expectations, chores,

expressions of respect, manners, and daily regimens designed to instill order and stability into the family-of-one structure as well as to provide a "you-can-count-on-it" foundation for each person in your extended family.

Check the elements which will help you establish discipline and responsibility
- ❑ maintain a regular time for study
- ❑ pick up after yourself
- ❑ do your share in washing dishes
- ❑ communicate with roommates
- ❑ do your own laundry
- ❑ call your family regularly
- ❑ allow suitemates to hold me accountable
- ❑ spend time with friends

4. Give selflessly to others.
We learn at a very early age to be possessive. "What I have is mine and you can't have it!" "What you have is mine and you can't take it!" Selfless giving builds self-esteem, security, and devotion. God has given us our family to love and cherish. "When we give of ourselves, we always receive more in return." Is this previous statement true or false from your perspective? ❑ True ❑ False

To demonstrate a Christlike character (to be an imitator of Christ) you need to demonstrate selfless giving as Christ did.
❑ True   ❑ False   Why or why not?

To acknowledge that your lifestyle will be different when you enter college is easy to do. However, understanding the idea of a "family of one" is sometimes harder. We falsely think "family" is something that happens after we get married and have kids. One day that may happen. However, the quality of your family begins with you developing the basics in your own life. Your room-mates, teachers, administrators, and friends on campus...they can help you build a strong family of one.

Steps to Discovering the Winning Edge
1. Spend quality time together with your family.
2. Keep the lines of communication open between yourself and others.
3. Maintain standards related to discipline and responsibility to one another.
4. Give selflessly to others.

Back 2 U
As a member of an extended family on campus, how important is it to you regarding how other students treat you?
What can you do to demonstrate a Christlike character in your own life this week?

[1]Branon, Dave. "Catching Up With... ." *Sports Spectrum*, May 1994, 29.

Day 2: Spiritual Disciplines That Last

Principle: Committed faith focuses on the basics.

Kyle developed some important spiritual disciplines as a boy. He read his Bible almost every night before going to bed. He often prayed during the day and would usually volunteer to pray aloud at church, which he rarely missed. But something happened during his first semester in college. He neglected these disciplines. Before long, other trouble signs began to show up in his life. Had it not been for his friends, Kyle would have easily drifted away. Now he's back on track in his Christian walk.

If someone asked you, "What basics are important to your college life?" how would you respond? Let the list be your guide. Check all that apply.

❏ eating	❏ sleeping	❏ studying
❏ hanging out	❏ entertainment	❏ playing
❏ hygiene	❏ good grades	❏ Greek involvement
❏ church	❏ friends	❏ attending class

What if you were asked, "What basics are important to your faith?" How would you answer?

You will find three spiritual guidelines that are a part of virtually every beginner's manual for new Christians:

- Read your Bible everyday.
- Pray everyday.
- Attend church regularly.

The basics. We all know at some level that we should do these things. But few of us actually do them. Unfortunately, some students begin to think that they are so mature that they don't need to do these things.

What do the basics do for us? When we read our Bibles daily:

- ✐ We become familiar with the whole of God's Word.
- ✐ We see the broader context and themes of God's truth.
- ✐ Familiar passages become imbedded in memory.
- ✐ By knowing what the Bible says, it is possible to apply Scripture. with greater accuracy and impact to daily circumstances.
- ✐ The Spirit of God begins to call to our remembrance what we have planted in our minds and hearts.
- ✐ The Word of God becomes a priority to us. In many ways, it becomes part of the way we think and respond.

Now <u>underline</u> the statements above which are

important basics in your life now. Circle the statements that reflect a need for improvement in your life.

If we don't know what the Bible has to say, we are in danger of turning to weaker belief systems for our values, which in turn have great potential for causing us to manifest arrogance, fear, doubt, anger, and pride. Would these help you discover the winning edge in life? No!

To live the best quality of life, we need to base our behaviors, thoughts, words, and responses on the best quality values. And those values are found in the Bible. To know the values of the Bible, we must read and study the Bible on a regular basis.

In the space below, rewrite your memory verse...even if you need to go back to Day 1 and review it. _____

_____

_____

When we are in daily communication with the Lord, it is much easier to express all of our emotions and ideas to Him. Kyle knew this and strayed away from the spiritual basics in his life. From the case study, if he did not have friends to guide him, where would he have gone spiritually? Put a "T" beside the statements you feel are true and a "F" beside those statements that you feel are false.

Without his friends, Kyle would

_____ have had a great time in college.

_____ would have experienced failure in all that he did.

_____ would have been closer to God.

_____ realized Bible study and prayer were not important.

_____ missed experiencing God's plan for his life.

Spiritual Basics

1. Have you seen or heard of an example when a student experienced an answer to a prayer in his or her life?   ❏ Yes   ❏ No
If you answered yes, write down your example in the space below.

2. When we attend church regularly, we build Christ-centered relationships as we are in fellowship with others. We find our time priorities coming into focus as church attendance and participation in other church functions become an important part of our schedules. *In an age of isolation and an eroding sense of friendship among people,*

70

regular church attendance can become the very thing that keeps us from living lonely, isolated lives. When tough times come, we have a support group already in place. We don't have to build a network with others. We have one.

In your own experience as a student, what have been some of the benefits of attending church regularly? _____

_____

Read the Scripture passage to the right, then answer the following questions: What is the "Book of the Law?" _____ "This Book
_____ of the Law shall
What should we do with this book? _____ not depart from
_____ your mouth, but
How often? _____ you shall meditate
Why? _____ in it day and
_____ night, that you
What are the results? _____ may observe to do
according to all
Based on your answers to these questions, how do you that is written
measure up to the standard in this verse? Place an **✗** on in it."
the line to indicate where you are now. —Joshua 1:8

Doing Great   **Need some improvement**   **Help**

_____

John 15:7 says: "If you abide in Me, and My words abide in you, you will ask what you desire, and it shall be done for you." What if one of your friends read this verse to you and said, "See, this is a blank check for me to get anything from God that I want." How would you respond? _____

_____

_____

Read Acts 2:1, 42, 46-47. Then, in the space below, identify the basic aspects of the early believers' worship experience. _____

_____

_____

If you asked polling experts today which team they believe is one of the best in high school football in America, many would, no doubt, name the team coached by Nick Hyder in Valdosta, Georgia. In the past decade, Hyder's teams have won more games than any other team in the nation. They have been named national champions four times and have won more than 20 state championships.

At the beginning of one of their practice sessions,

71

a young aspiring coach went to Valdosta to watch Coach Hyder in action. He wanted to see what kind of practices the coach conducted, hoping to pick up a few game winning tips. He found the practices were well organized but boring to watch. They involved little more than hours of drills in blocking, tackling, throwing, catching, and kicking––the basics of football. The new coach thought to himself, "This is a lot like a Pop Warner practice––just a lot of work every day on the basics."

At the conclusion of the week, the young coach went to Coach Hyder to thank him for the privilege of watching his practices. He said, "One thing I don't understand, Coach. You spent all of your practice time doing things your players should have mastered years ago. Are you in a rebuilding year?"

"No," Coach Hyder replied.

"Wow!" the young coach said. "Then why all the emphasis on practice in the basics?"

Coach Hyder answered, "Do you want to know the secret of my coaching success? That's why you came, isn't it? Let me tell you. The winning football teams always do the basic things the best––blocking, tackling, throwing, catching, and kicking. The more talented the athlete, the easier it is to get away from the basics. But it's skill in the basics that wins games."

If you look at people you consider to be spiritually mighty and powerful today, it is likely that they pray frequently, study the Bible diligently, and are in constant fellowship with other Christians. They haven't moved beyond the basics. If anything, they are spending more time on the basics than on anything else.

As a student, make the basics a part of your daily spiritual walk. When crisis hits others, you will be spiritually fit to leap into action. When a crisis hits your life you will have a firm spiritual foundation and faith-filled friends. Spiritual disciplines are necessary to adopt, to grow, and to mature in Christ's likeness.

Steps to Discovering the Winning Edge
1. Read your Bible on a regular basis.
2. Pray every day.
3. Attend church regularly.

Back 2 U
Are the basics important in discovering the winning edge? Name one spiritual disciple you need in your life? What actions can you take to further develop your own spiritual disciplines?

Day 3: Spiritual Power to Grow

Principle: Committed faith focuses on the basics.

Rebecca lost her grandmother six months ago. She is now studying hard for a test she fears she might not pass. Both experiences are "bummers." Rebecca has grown in her faith and is now putting into practice God's strength in her life. With the death of her grandmother, it has been hard and there have been many tears, but God has made a way for her to demonstrate His strength. As she studies, she prays for His strength again to give her the clarity she needs to be successful on the test.

As the psalmist prayed, "Strengthen me according to Your word" (Ps. 119:28), so must we. All that we do as Christians is with the strength God provides (see 1 Pet. 4:11). The apostle Paul prayed to God on behalf of the Christians in Ephesus "that He would grant you, according to the riches of His glory, to be strengthened with might through His Spirit in the inner man" (Eph. 3:16). Wow! Just think, as a student you don't have to be Superman. You find your strength to conquer the temptations and negative influence because of your relationship to Christ.

Using the phrase SPIRITUAL POWER in an acrostic, develop a definition of what God provides for each of us. Support as many letters as possible with a Scripture reference.

S _____ P _____
P _____ O _____
I Integrity (Prov. 11:3)   W _____
R _____ E _____
I _____ R _____
T _____
U _____
A _____
L _____

Read Daniel 3. What actions demonstrated that these three young men relied upon God's spiritual power? _____
_____
_____
_____

As a student, when the basics are in place in our lives, crises can be faced no matter what they look like or how they come into our lives. We claim spiritual power!

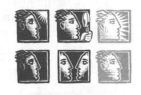

To review, see if you can list the three basic elements of spiritual growth mentioned in yesterday's study. If you can't remember, go back to yesterday's "steps."

R_____

P_____

A_____

Strong in the Lord

Read Ephesians 6:10-19. The apostle Paul was addressing the church at Ephesus concerning the basics of Christian behavior. His first point emphasized being _____ in the Lord (see Eph. 6:10).

Paul went on to describe in verses 13-19 how the believers could continue to stay strong in the Lord. He told them to put on the whole armor of God. The armor was spiritual in nature and it involved these elements:

- truth
- righteousness
- the gospel of peace
- faith
- salvation
- the Word of God

Although Paul gives reference to a battle, as a student you probably aren't involved in many battles. So, why would you need "armor?" Because you do face emotional, psychological, intellectual, and spiritual battles every day on campus. Do you believe this? ❑ Yes ❑ No
List one or two reasons for the answer you gave in the box.
1.
2.

What were the Ephesians to do once they were fully armed for spiritual battle? They were to pray and be on continual alert against evil, to stand with perseverance and boldness. Yet again, the basics.

Paul gives us a spiritual prescription for taking on all that Satan throws our way. He instructs us to "Be strong in the Lord and in the power of His might" (Eph. 6:10). Paul then outlines a course of action that will insure spiritual power.

Complete the following chart by placing an example of what each word represents for you as a student when you put on "the whole armor of God."

armor _____

belt of truth _____

breastplate _____

shield of faith _____

helmet of salvation _____

sword of the Spirit _____

After Paul instructs us to put on the full armor of God, he then gives us guidance about when and how we should pray (v. 18). Based on Paul's model, reflect on your own prayer life then answer the following questions:

When do you usually pray? _____

_____

What kind of prayers do you pray? _____

_____

Who can you pray for today? _____

_____

What can you ask God to do for that person today? How would you want another believer to pray for you? _____

_____

During the early 1990s, Dana Drew was no doubt the leader of the University of Toledo ladies' basketball team. Voted "Mid-American Conference Player of the Year" on more than one occasion, she earned Academic All-American first team honors and was voted co-president of her Fellowship of Christian Athletes (FCA) chapter, just to name a few of her accomplishments.

In spite of all of her accomplishments, however, Dana understood the pressures of the college scene. Although it wasn't easy to reject these pressures, her spiritual disciplines took her to the high road.

"I think there's a lot of things that reaffirm my belief in Jesus Christ. You can probably look at them as pressures. But you can also look at them as opportunities. Taking a situation that you might be put in, that could possibly be pressure, but instead turning it around and asking Him for strength and support."

"And through prayer, turning that into an opportunity to reach out and touch someone's life. Or if you are in a position to be a good role model, someone might see you and say, 'Hey, look, she's not doing that!' or, 'She's different. What makes her different?' And then you have to have the opportunity to say, 'It's Jesus Christ in my life that

makes me different.' So I hope that instead of looking at it as pressure, I would look at it as an opportunity to share my faith."[1]

> ➤ A coach knows a player is courting disaster when he begins to rely on his athletic prowess to the neglect of the basics.
> ➤ A college student begins to run into danger when she starts trusting her instincts and throws all standard study principles aside.
> ➤ An engaged couple flirts with disaster when he or she takes a relationship for granted and stops doing the basics related to romance, appreciation, and expressions of love.
> ➤ Students put themselves into the danger zone when they stop taking spiritual basics seriously in their lives.

And in our spiritual lives, as a student we are opening ourselves up to evil itself when we say, "I am too busy today to read God's Word. I'll do it tomorrow." "I don't have time today to pray. God will understand." "It's all right if I don't go to church this Sunday. I don't need to go every Sunday. I can miss a time or two."

Stick to the basics. Stay after them. Immerse yourself in them. They are the keys to building up all of the inner resources necessary to acquire and maintain spiritual power.

Today, I will work to develop spiritual power in my life by _____

_____

_____

Steps to Discovering the Winning Edge
1. Recognize that God provides the spiritual power we need as Christians.
2. We stay strong in the Lord when we put on the "whole armor of God."
3. When the basics are in place, the winning edge will be apparent throughout our lives.

Back 2 U
Do you think Rebecca's prayer before the test was a waste of time?
What is the one thing you remember from this session?
Do you feel you can grow spiritually?
How can you experience the winning edge through the practice
of spiritual basics in your life?

[1]Spencer, Heather. "Not Just a Passing Fancy." *Sports Spectrum*, November 1994, 9.

Day 4: Commitment Leads to Action

Principle: Committed faith focuses on the basics.

Travis stayed focused all through his undergraduate work. Now in his final year of his master's program, Travis is finally seeing the light at the end of the tunnel. Whenever he is discouraged and down, he repeats what his pastor had shared with him five years earlier, "Commitment leads to action." Travis relies on his commitment to complete his study to the best of his ability.

The ability to set goals is one trail that sets you as a student apart from all other creatures. A goal is different from a dream. A dream is a picture of the world the way we want it to be or as it should be. A goal is a picture of the world the way you are willing to work to make it become.

The path from dream to development of a plan requires commitment. Commitment is a belief in yourself and the worthiness of your effort. In many ways, commitment is obedience to the plan. It is staying dedicated to the thing that you want to accomplish and doing everything within your power to marshal your resources toward a positive result.

Check the goal development lines. Choose two goals and write one above each line. Then on each line determine where you are in reaching that goal. Put an ✗ on the line to indicate at which step you have arrived.

Dream   Plan Development   Commitment   Action

_____

_____

Remember, it's not where the mark is now, it's where you are headed.

A Man with a Dream
Joshua had a dream of living in the promised land. He was one of the two spies who had returned from Canaan with a positive report. For 40 years of wandering through the wilderness, Joshua kept that dream alive that he might one day live in the land flowing with milk and honey, a land he described as, "exceedingly good."

The day came when the dream was about to be turned into a goal.

Read Joshua 1:1-9 and then be prepared to answer the following questions. What four goals did the Lord present to Joshua?

1._____

2._____

3._____

4._____

Notice that the goals were stated in far more specific terms than the dreams: "go over this Jordan," "every place that the sole of your foot will tread upon," "you shall divide as an inheritance the land," and "observe to do according to all the law."

Joshua knew that to realize the dream, he had to mobilize the people to cross, walk, and divide the land, keeping the law of Moses as they went.

What did the Lord say three times to Joshua?

_____

Three times, the Lord said to Joshua, "Be strong, and of good courage." The Lord knew that for the goal to be reached, Joshua was going to have to stay committed and keep his faith focused.

The goal was then turned into a plan. Joshua commanded the people to prepare provisions. He told which people to remain east of the Jordan. He sent two men to spy out the land, especially Jericho.

When the two spies returned, they said to Joshua, "Truly the Lord has delivered all the land into our hands, for indeed all the inhabitants of the country are fainthearted because of us" (Josh. 2:24).

Joshua led the people across the Jordan; and on the other side, the Lord gave Joshua the rest of His plan for conquering Jericho. The priests and the armed men with the covenant would march around the city for six days. On the seventh day, they were commanded to march around the city seven times, blow the trumpets, and shout.

If you had been Joshua, do you think this plan would have much merit?
❏ Yes   ❏ No

On the seventh day, as the trumpets blared and the people shouted, "The wall fell down flat" (Josh. 6:20). The people rushed into the city and utterly destroyed all that was in it except for Rahab and her family.

Joshua's focus on what God had given him--a dream,

78

then his goal, and then his plan--eventually paid off.

Psalm 37:5 reads, "Commit your way to the Lord, trust also in Him, and He shall bring it to pass."

God desires for us to commit ourselves to Him and to trust in Him. If we are found faithful in these two basic principles of the Christian life, then God promises to be Lord of our lives.

Are you committed to the Lord Jesus Christ? Are you trusting in Him with every decision of your life? As a student, every day you are challenged by God to commit yourself to Him and to trust Him. In the space below, put an ✗ in the boxes that reflect areas of your life in which you need to trust God more or commit to Him.

❑ reading the Bible daily   ❑ attending church regularly
❑ learning to study better   ❑ knowing God is on my side
❑ overcoming inferiority feelings   ❑ developing strong Christian
❑ sharing Christ with others   character
❑ learning more about God   ❑ developing quality relationships
❑ standing up for my faith   ❑ spending more time in prayer

Don't let any obstacles stand in your way and keep you from pursuing the dreams God has planted in your heart. Don't let the actions of others keep you from doing your best, giving your utmost, and experiencing the winning edge.

Consider the following poem:

GIVE YOUR BEST
People are unreasonable, illogical, and self-centered. Love them anyway.
If you do good, people will accuse you of selfish, ulterior motives. Do good anyway.
If you are successful, you will win false friends and true enemies. Succeed anyway.
Honesty and frankness make you vulnerable. Be honest and frank anyway.
The good you do today will be forgotten tomorrow. Do good anyway.
The biggest people with the biggest ideas can be shot down by the smallest people with the smallest minds. Think big anyway.
People favor underdogs but follow only top dogs. Fight for some underdogs anyway.
What you spend years building may be destroyed overnight. Build anyway.
Give the world the best you have, and you will get kicked in the teeth. Give the world the best you've got anyway.
--Author unknown

Stay focused. Do what you know to do, are called to do, and believe is right to do. Stay focused and persist, no matter what others do.

Go back to the case study and ask yourself this question, "What had Travis learned in life which would allow him to be at the point of discovering the winning edge?" Write down at least two things you see in his life that a successful Christian will exhibit on a daily basis.

1._____

2._____

What Travis has, you can have, too. Today, I will commit and trust God by

_____

_____

Steps to Discovering the Winning Edge
1. The path from dream to plan requires commitment and action.
2. Do what you know to do, are called to do, and believe is right to do.
3. Commit yourself to God and trust in Him, and then He will act.

Back 2 U
In what ways has Travis made a commitment to the winning edge?
For you to be more committed and trusting, what must you give up?
How can other students discover the winning edge in their lives?

Day 5: Confronting the Intimidators

Principle: Committed faith focuses on the basics.

> In high school, Ryan always seemed to know what to do in order to be "escorted" to the principal's office for his bi-weekly "talk" due to his behavior in class. Now in college, Ryan received a memo to "Please see Dean Warren in his office this afternoon." His old fears have resurfaced. However, this time he received word that the professors in his major division had awarded him the "Outstanding Student Award" for the year. No more intimidation.

Who intimidates you? For each person, place an ✗ in the appropriate column.

	Always	Sometimes	Never
• security guard	_____	_____	_____
• dentist	_____	_____	_____
• dean of students	_____	_____	_____
• girlfriend/boyfriend	_____	_____	_____
• college president	_____	_____	_____
• professor	_____	_____	_____
• athletes	_____	_____	_____
• fraternity/sorority members	_____	_____	_____
• pastor	_____	_____	_____
• friends	_____	_____	_____

It's important to realize that intimidators are all around you as a student. However, it's also important to realize a person becomes intimidating only because one allows himself to become intimidated.

What does the word "intimidate" really mean? It means to "make timid—to fill with fear, to overawe, to deter by discouraging." Intimidation causes people to cower, to struggle against something they suspect is bigger and more powerful than they are.

Look at the list below. Draw a box around the qualities of an "intimidator." Draw a circle around the qualities of an "encourager."

winning
cooperation
mutual satisfaction
competition
power
joint decision making
control

Intimidators who consciously and purposely intend to intimidate others nearly always emphasize one or more of these elements: control, competition, winning, and power.

Few people thrive in an environment or a relationship in which winning and power are emphasized constantly. On the other hand, most people are comfortable and relaxed in environments marked by these qualities: cooperation, mutual satisfaction, and joint decision making.

Encouragers look for win-win situations rather than one-winner-takes-all situations. Encouragers seek cooperation rather than competition. Encouragers respect and value others rather than putting them down. Encouragers are not necessarily emotionally weak or indecisive people. On the contrary, they are often very strong and effective leaders, with bold ideas and creative solutions gained in part through their ability to interact with others. Encouragers are far more popular than intimidators, a factor that tends to benefit them greatly because people open up to them and give them ideas and suggestions that they can use to help others.

Write down some of the actions encouragers take:

_____
_____
_____

Read Ephesians 5:15-20. What four actions does Paul encourage the Ephesians to take that build encourager qualities in one's life?
1._____
2._____
3._____
4._____

How to Develop Encourager Qualities
• *First, choose to associate with encouragers.* Marry an encourager, attend a church led by an encourager, work for an encourager, and hire encouragers.

• *Second, refuse to compete or play the compare game with an intimidator.* Suggest cooperation to the person privately, and if the person refuses that option, suggest cooperation to the person in the presence of a third party who is willing to cooperate.

• *Third, turn your eyes away from the intimidator and find someone that you might encourage.* A number of psychologists advise their depressed clients to make someone else feel good as a part of their therapy. Make it a priority in your life to encourage someone

else. Find someone on campus to encourage as often as possible--maybe your roommate.

Read Acts 6 and 7. As you read these two chapters, be looking for the answers to fill in the blanks below to help you understand Stephen's experience.

Stephen, "full of _____ and _____" (6:8) was charged with being a blasphemer. Stephen addressed the accusers in such a way that they "saw his face as a face of an angel." They were not able to resist the _____ and the _____by which he spoke (6:10). Stephen spoke with assurance that came in knowing he was speaking what God would have him to say.

The fact is, the intimidators became the intimidated. Stephen's accusers were intimidated by Stephen, who was full of the _____ _____ (7:55) as he preached to them. Stephen was _____ to death (7:59) by those who attempted to intimidate him. You may say, "Well, that sounds like defeat to me." Stephen and all those in the early church didn't see it that way. They saw it as a great victory.

> **When we stand for right, the Lord stands with us--**
> **both now and for all eternity.**

Winning-Edge Principles
What must we do when we come face to face with people who intimidate us?

• *We must learn to stand up!*
That doesn't automatically mean we won't have to pay a price. We may be persecuted. That was the case for Dave Williams. A tackle for the Houston Oilers, Dave missed a game a few seasons back because he chose to stay with his wife as she gave birth to their son, Scott. The team fined him $110,000 for missing the game. On a nationally-televised show, program host Connie Chung asked him about paying $110,000 to be with his wife in the delivery room. Williams said, "There isn't enough money in the world to trade for that moment. Family comes first." Chung asked him, "If the fine had been for a million dollars, would you have still missed the game?" He said, "Yes." Dave Williams may have lost some money, but he retained his principles.

• *There is no victory in compromising values.*
Many things can be compromised--differences regarding methods, schedules, priorities, style, location. But if you compromise your values to gain a temporary victory for yourself, you lose in the long run. One of the main things you lose is your integrity. And right behind it are your courage and your faith. As a student, you must never compromise your belief in what is right, especially when you have a deep

heartfelt assurance that it is right in God's sight and according to God's Word. Know with certainty that what you believe is in God's Word and that you understand God's Word in the full context of its meaning.

You have the Lord on your side. You may be persecuted in the process, but you will not fail.

As I overcome intimidators in my life today, I will _____
_____
_____
_____

Steps to Discovering the Winning Edge
1. A person intimidates you only because you allow yourself to become intimidated.
2. Be sure that what you stand for is what Jesus Christ stands for.
3. No one wins by compromising his values.

Back 2 U
No more fear!
Have you experienced this feeling? Would you like to?
Do you think Dave Williams did the right thing?
Do you have to conquer the intimidators
to discover the winning edge?

Winning Through Perseverance

Day 1: Carelessness Costs

Principle: Endurance wins over temporary setbacks.

Colleen had been dating her boyfriend for more than a year now. They had become a regular item around the campus during lunch breaks and evening walks. During a recent disagreement, Colleen reminded her boyfriend of a tasteless comment he made a year ago. Their relationship is being challenged now because of one careless comment.

The cost of carelessness can be high. Think of a time when you said or did something carelessly. What has it cost you? Here are some examples. You can add others.

- taking an exam and failing to read it over again before turning it in
- forgetting to type a complete bibliography on a term paper
- failing to write down a key point during a lecture
- being late for a class because you overslept
- being overdrawn in your checkbook after failing to record an entry

Below are five causes of carelessness. After reading the information *below each cause, check the box that most accurately describes you and how you are currently dealing with each cause.*

Cause 1: IMPATIENCE
Sometimes carelessness stems from impatience. We look for a faster, easier way to get a job done. Take your time. Be diligent. Don't try to cram too much into your schedule.

❏ I can never wait.
❏ I am cautiously patient.
❏ I am relatively patient.
❏ Patience is my virtue.

Has impatience affected your lifestyle on campus?
❑ Yes ❑ No ❑ Sometimes

Cause 2: GREED

Sometimes a desire for unnecessary gain can drive us toward carelessness. A need to have "it" and have "it" now dictates our lives. Our needs and wants can be dictated by selfish greed.

❑ If I want it, I will get it.
❑ I'll wait, but not long.
❑ I can probably wait.
❑ I can do without it.

Has greed affected your lifestyle on campus? ❑ Yes ❑ No ❑ Sometimes

Cause 3: DISTRACTIONS

Sometimes a distraction can cause us to lose our direction and focus. We can become disoriented which can cause us to be careless. Staying alert and paying close attention to what we are doing keeps us focused and sharp.

❑ I get distracted easily.
❑ At times I may get distracted.
❑ I try not to get distracted.
❑ I mostly stay focused and alert.

Have distractions affected your lifestyle on campus?
❑ Yes ❑ No ❑ Sometimes

Cause 4: BAD ADVICE

Sometimes we make decisions based on bad advice we receive from others. There are times we need to seek wise counsel from others. It is wise for us, however, to take the time to check that advice with another person or get a second opinion.

❑ I seem to always act on bad advice.
❑ At times I listen to bad advice.
❑ I usually get advice from wise people.
❑ I always make decisions based on wise counsel.

Has bad advice affected your lifestyle on campus?
❑ Yes ❑ No ❑ Sometimes

Cause 5: WRONG ASSUMPTIONS

Sometimes our assumptions can get us into trouble.

We may assume something to be one way, when
actually it is the other way. Our assumptions can be misleading and careless.

❑ I tend to always make wrong assumptions.
❑ Occasionally, I may make a wrong assumption.
❑ I rarely follow through on a wrong assumption.
❑ I never act on wrong assumptions.

Have wrong assumptions affected your lifestyle on campus?
❑ Yes   ❑ No   ❑ Sometimes

Check the marks you made in the boxes. Do they show a pattern of how you
are living your life? If you see a pattern of carelessness in your life caused by
impatience, greed, distractions, bad advice, and wrong assumptions, you don't
have to live that way. Some giants we create for ourselves by what we do.
Others we create by what we don't do. All our giants can be put behind us
through Christ's real love in our lives.

Five Steps to Getting on Track
When we do the five things in the following list, we put ourselves on
track where we are less likely to face the totally unexpected, devastating
problems that can prevent us from experiencing the winning edge which
God wants to give us.
1. Take your time. Do every task in your life with diligence and care.
2. Pay the price. Don't be enticed by greed or easy-money ploys.
3. Stay focused. Don't allow yourself to be distracted when engaged in
a task that has any degree of danger associated with it.
4. Check out the advice people give you. Obtain at least two opinions
from people you respect before taking a major step.
5. Don't assume. Be sure.

When we are careless and the consequences of our carelessness result in problems, we nearly always think less of ourselves. If you become the victim of
your own carelessness:
- Apologize to any person you have hurt, including yourself. Don't try to
justify what you have done. Admit your fault.
- Make amends as best you can. Sometimes that might mean paying for
damages. It may even mean community service. Penitence is not necessarily something to be avoided. It can be part of the healing for other
victims. Penitence also puts one in a position to truly forgive oneself.
- Make a change in your habits. Recognize the
element of carelessness that leads to the problem and work hard at changing the way you go
about doing things.
- Share your carelessness with Christ through
prayer.

Read Ephesians 4:20-24. The apostle Paul challenges us how we should live. Instead of having to suffer the consequences of careless acts, Paul first writes "You have not so learned Christ, if indeed you have heard Him and have been taught by Him, as the truth is in Jesus" (vv. 20-21).

Rewrite verse 22 in your own words _____
_____
_____

Are you allowing God to renew you "in the spirit of your mind" as verse 23 states? How should such a renewal affect the way you live at this point in your life?_____
_____

How does God's will help us avoid the causes of carelessness discussed earlier?
_____
_____

Take care in order to stay strong. Feed your spirit, mind, and body with the right nourishment. Develop habits that build character and result in success. You'll be in a much stronger position as a student––to enjoy times of peace and harmony in your life and survive times of crisis.

Have you discovered the secret of successful living? Are you making the most of every opportunity as Paul exhorted in Ephesians 5:16?

Carelessness costs! Today, I will examine at least one way I can avoid being the victim of carelessness by_____
_____

Steps to Discovering the Winning Edge
1. Avoid the causes of carelessness: impatience, greed, distractions, bad advice, and wrong assumptions.
2. Live a wise and careful life, making the most of every opportunity.
3. God's will is for us to be a new self, created to be like God.

Back 2 U
Have you been the victim of a careless word?
Has your life been "ruled" by the five cause of carelessness?
What steps can you take to become new in Christ and
discover the winning edge to life?

Day 2: Renewing the Mind

Principle: Endurance wins over temporary setbacks.

Verse to Memorize This Week: Do not be conformed to this world, but be transformed by the renewing of your mind, that you may prove what is that good and acceptable and perfect will of God."--Romans 12:2

> Josh never considered himself to be someone who had a "dirty mind." He never told dirty jokes, but he wouldn't walk away when one was being told. Josh knew that he was compromising his integrity. Some of the music he listened to could also be labeled as comprising, however, he actually favored contemporary Christian music. Josh struggled most with his selection of movies, especially the ones he rented. They were far from helping him to renew his mind.

Open Book Test

In Romans 12:2, Paul provides 12 powerful words that help one experience a renewing of the mind. Renewing the mind is essential in discovering the winning edge for life. See if you can identify at least six of these words and put them on the lines below:

1. _____
2. _____
3. _____
4. _____
5. _____
6. _____

(If you are doing this exercise with a group, feel free to compare your answers.)

As Christian students, we need to be aware and concerned about the pollution of our minds, our attitudes, and our value systems. The freedom many people experience on campus also opens the door to many temptations. Such temptations can lead to the pollution of people's minds. Mind pollution is not just limited to what comes from television, videos, magazines, radios, or newspapers. Much of the pollution can come from friends, what is heard in the classroom, and social activities in which one is bombarded by mes ges that tell people they're worthless, incompetent, without a future, and oi little value.

Look at Romans 12:2 again. Identify three actions which reflect the pattern for living a fruitful Christian life.

1. _____
2. _____
3. _____

How can we go about cleaning up our minds?

Evaluate how these suggestions impact your life by putting a circle around the number representing where you are on a scale of 1-10, with "1" being "a major problem" and "10" being "not a problem."

FIRST: TURN OFF THE FLOW

We begin by turning off the in-flow of poisons and trash. Control what is heard and read and viewed in your room and in social settings. Refuse to watch any behavior that you don't want to emulate. Refuse to listen to lyrics that depict behavior that you wouldn't want to do or have done to you.

1	2	3	4	5	6	7	8	9	10

A major problem   Sometimes a problem   Not a problem

SECOND: ASK FOR GOD'S HELP

Ask the Lord to cleanse your mind. Ask Him to drive away any remembrance of the negative images and words you have taken into your life. Ask Him to free you from any nightmares you may have experienced as a result of your polluting behavior. Ask Him to forgive you for putting your focus on things that are unlike Him and are unworthy of His people.

1	2	3	4	5	6	7	8	9	10

A major problem   Sometimes a problem   Not a problem

THIRD: TAKE IN THE POSITIVE

Start putting into your mind positive thoughts, affirmations, music, and images. Choose to be renewed in your mind.

1	2	3	4	5	6	7	8	9	10

A major problem   Sometimes a problem   Not a problem

FOURTH: REALIZE THE "IZE" HAVE IT

- MEMORIZE at least one great truth everyday. It may be an inspiring poem, an especially helpful verse of Scripture, an affirmation, or a favorite quotation. What you memorize becomes a part of your life, your character, and your future.

- CRYSTALLIZE your goals, your aspirations, and your ambitions. Write them down and include a workable timetable for their accomplishment.

- SPECIALIZE in some particular field. Become an expert and you will soon become indispensable. Become an authority, and you will inevitably become sought after.

- NEUTRALIZE your fears, your doubts, and your anxieties through the power of prayer, meditation, and a positive mental attitude.

- MINIMIZE your shortcomings, your liabilities, and your deficiencies. Because you were designed by a Master Architect, you are greater than you think.

- MAXIMIZE your abilities, your talents, your potentialities, and your possibilities. Accentuate your positives.

- RECOGNIZE the good in others, the beauty of friendship, the splendor of love, and the joy of service. Train your eyes to look for the best in others, and invariably, others will see the best in you.

Can you remember the four ways to clean up your mind? Write them below.

T _____

A _____

T _____

I_____

A Renewed Mind

Write down some ways students can demonstrate a renewed mind as a member of the various organizations or groups below. Fill in those which apply. You are given extra lines to indicate your own choices of a group.

Fraternity or sorority?

_____

_____

Athletic team?

_____

_____

Music ensemble?

_____

_____

Student government body?

_____

_____

Local church?

_____

_____

(Please indicate other—   )

_____

_____

91

Many people haven't come to this realization: You can choose your attitude. You aren't born with the attitude you have today. You acquire it. And if you have acquired a bad attitude, you can change it and acquire a good one.

There is a story of two shoe salesmen who were sent to a newly-discovered Pacific island inhabited by primitive natives. Upon arriving, Salesperson A called his home office and said, "Send the company plane down here right away and get me out of this place. There's no shoe business here. The natives are running around barefoot!"

Salesperson B, on the other hand, called the home office with a radically different message: "Hey, boss, I have found us a bonanza! Rush me all the shoes you can—all sizes, all styles, all colors. These poor natives are running around barefoot!"

Both salespeople faced the same circumstances. One chose to see a potential for good; the other saw only bad.

Because God gives me the power to obtain a renewed mind, today, I will_____
_____
_____

Steps to Discovering the Winning Edge
1. Cleaning up our minds involves turning off the flow of trash, asking God for help, and taking in the positive.
2. If you want to know who you are, evaluate what you think about yourself.
3. We are what we think about.

Back 2 U
In what ways can you relate to Josh in the case study?
What steps can you implement in your life on campus to renew your mind?
If you were a friend of Josh, how do you think
you could help him with his problems?
How close are you to discovering the winning edge?

Day 3: Keeping Clean Thoughts

Principle: Endurance wins over temporary setbacks.

> Brooke seemed like any other girl around the guys. She was well liked, attended many campus ministry activities, and fit in well with most groups. However, when she was with the girls on her dorm floor, she would tell racially- and sexually-insulting jokes. Everyone laughed, but felt ashamed after awhile. No one had the courage to confront her.

Read the following seven Scripture references and match each item by drawing a line to its appropriate action.

1 Thessalonians 5:11	Rid myself of filthy language
James 4:12	Be a blessing to others
Colossians 3:8	Create in me a clean heart
Philippians 2:4	Build each other up
James 1:21	Rid myself of all moral filth
Romans 1:12	Be interested in others
Psalm 51:10	Avoid finding fault with others

Choose one of these verses and write it on the line below. Commit yourself to memorize this verse. _____

_____

_____

Choose to be around people who point out the positive, speak truth, are kind, and have a gentle spirit. You'll be healthy attitudinally.

Impure Thoughts

No matter how hard you try, you will be confronted with impure thoughts. As a student, if you are alive, you will have temptations and impure thoughts all around you. If you are suffering from mind pollution, you may need to move to a cleaner environment. That doesn't mean you need to relocate physically, although that may be advisable in some instances. It does mean you may need to find new friends and make new associations. You may need to change your relationship environment. Based on your present relationships on campus, and being as honest as you can, would you say you need to "relocate?"

❑ Yes   ❑ No   ❑ Maybe

Why? _____

_____

_____

_____

It is difficult to maintain a clean and healthy thought life if you are constantly around people who

- criticize others constantly, whether it's school administration, your roommate, others in the fraternity or other groups of people on campus such as band members. People who criticize nonstop spew toxic attitudes into your mind. Move away from them!
- tell lewd, rude, or racially- and culturally-biased jokes and stories. Even though they may be a friend, either refuse to join them or let them know you don't want this type of behavior to be characteristic of your friendship.
- routinely use profanity. As a student you are exposed to this every day. If it's not through media, it's through relationships, graffiti, and what you read. Move away!
- are insulting or mean spirited in what they say to you. Walk away from their insults. Don't let their words take root in you.

How do you measure up to each of these actions? Do you have a problem with...(Circle or underline the appropriate response to each situation.)
- ❑ Criticism? (No, Sometimes, Yes)
- ❑ Gutter talk? (No, Sometimes, Yes)
- ❑ Profanity? (No, Sometimes, Yes)
- ❑ Insults? (No, Sometimes, Yes)

Sexuality Under Attack
One of the places Satan attacks our Christian character and desires most easily is through our understanding and behavior related to sex. Satan attempts to stimulate impure thoughts which can, in turn, result in ungodly actions. For example, look at the list below. How would you score yourself on the following statements?

Place a "check mark" beside the statements that reflect activities you have participated in recently:
____ I have listened to sexually-explicit music in my dorm room.
____ I have seen a sexually-explicit movie with other students.
____ I have read a pornographic magazine in my dorm room.
____ I have talked crudely about sex with other students.
____ I have lusted after another woman/man and thought about having sex.
____ I have listened to off-color jokes because the person telling them was a friend.
____ I have told off-color jokes in order to be a part of the crowd on campus.
____ I have made inappropriate comments about another woman's/man's body.

One reaction you can have to this is, "Everyone on campus does it. No big deal!"

94

William Tillman, Jr., a professor at Southwestern Baptist Theological Seminary wrote, "The basic legal foundation for identifying pornography goes back to a Supreme Court decision in 1957, 'Roth vs. United States.' The essence of the decision was that a test for obscenity was whether an average person of the community could judge material to arouse lustfulness. Any form of media can convey obscenity. Still photographs, statues, books, movies, playing cards, slides, and records (tapes and compact discs) pedal pornography."[1]

Open dorms, gay dorms, erotica week, national coming out week, free material on the internet...Anyone can now openly express his or her sexual desires and most people don't care.

Tillman goes on to say, "For the Christian, there is no defense for pornography. Such material promotes a false, even damaging view of sexuality. Premarital and marital fidelity and chastity are undermined. Irresponsibility and promiscuity become norms."

But, what would happen if you as a Christian challenged the norms? What if you told Brooke in our case study that you didn't want to listen to her unChristian language? What if you took a stand for Christlike behavior?

The Bible and Sexuality
Pornography presents a view of sexuality and its relationship to all of life which is alien to the Bible. See, for example, Genesis 1:27-28; Exodus 20:14; Job 31:1; Matthew 5:27-28; 19:8-9; Romans 1:24-32; 1 Corinthians 6:13-20; Philippians 4:8-9."[2]

Read Mark 7:20-23 and see if you can answer the following questions.
What does Jesus say makes a person unclean? _____
_____

What are the "evils" that come from the heart? _____
_____

Read 2 Corinthians 10:4-5 and read about the alternative, according to Scripture. What does Paul mean when he refers to the "weapons of our warfare"?
_____
_____

What "power" do these weapons possess? _____
_____

What does it mean to you to take "bring every thought into captivity"?_____
_____

David was one of Israel's most famous kings. How easy it would have been to "glaze over" the realities of his inner life. Yet, Scripture tells us the later years of David's life were marred by an affair with Bathsheba. He first gazed upon her. Then he desired her and plotted to have her. His lust soon gave way to adultery. Much of the good David did in his life was soon overshadowed by giving in to unclean thoughts.

Only much later did David repent of his sin and draw close to God to find strength and forgiveness. Do you remember our discussion earlier in the study about forgiveness and being forgiven? David experienced God's forgiveness and became a new person. As the passage in 2 Corinthians 10:5 states, we bring "every thought into captivity to the obedience of Christ." You do have the power to take a stand!

Satan can use our thoughts and turn them into sinful actions. However, God has given us the power to overcome these thoughts. Our every thought can become "obedient to Christ." Are you willing to make this decision on a daily basis? ❏ Yes   ❏ No

Because of my desire to maintain clean thoughts, I will _____
_____
_____
_____

Steps to Discovering the Winning Edge
1. Stay away from people who criticize, tell rude jokes,
and use profanity and insults.
2. Choose to be around people who point out the positive,
speak truth, are kind, and have a gentle spirit.
3. Commit your thoughts to God and
take captive every thought to make it obedient to Christ.

Back 2 U
How could you share with Brooke your convictions without being offensive?
Why are our thoughts related to sexuality so important?
Can our thoughts help us discover the winning edge?

[1]*The Family Worship Bible*, New International Version (Nashville: Holman Bible Publishers, 1991), 1331.
[2]Ibid., 1331.

Day 4: Temporary Setbacks

Principle: Endurance wins over temporary setbacks.

> Brian is entering his senior year of college undecided about his career. Recently, he has become withdrawn from his family and friends. His grades have dropped, he has lost his appetite, and he has difficulty sleeping. His roommate has confronted him with these symptoms. Brian has agreed to see the school counselor and to begin working on his feelings.

What does a sand trap do to a golfer's score? You don't have to be a golfer to *guess the right answer.*

Landing in a sand trap sets back the score at least one stroke, especially if the sand trap is one that lines a fairway. In hitting out of a sand trap, a player has a little less control and a whole lot less power on the ball.

Are you aware that while you are a student, you will experience "sand traps?" *Life's sand traps come in at least four varieties:*

➤ Minor Setbacks
Some of life's sand traps come in the form of minor setbacks––an unexpected bill, a flat tire on the car, a tooth that needs filling, a bout with the flu, a poor test grade.

➤ Lack of Organization
Sometimes we get bogged down in the game of life because we let things get out of control. Our schedules, our environments, and our very lives lack organization so that we don't know which way to turn next.

Organizing is not limited to things. It includes organization of time and resources. Part of reorganizing our lives for success should involve delegating various chores or tasks that we have taken on and are bogging us down.

➤ Bad Habits
Nearly all of us can identify one or more bad habits that slow us down, trip us up, or keep us from reaching our full potential. If bad habits aren't faced and dealt with, they can become addictions, obsessions, or illnesses.

➤ Depression
Perhaps the most insidious sand trap of all is the deep discouragement and despair that we know as depression. Depression comes in many varieties, from feeling a little down on a particular day to clinical depression

that sometimes results in hospitalization. If you find yourself depressed, take time to visit the health or counseling center on campus. These feelings are treatable. There's no "shame or guilt" in desiring good health and doing what is needed to obtain it.

Overcoming Depression

1) Find a way to express your inner feelings (write them down or talk to a friend).
2) Envision a future you want to have and is realistic for you to obtain.
3) Accept the prayers of others and believe that God will answer both their prayers and your own prayers for your future well-being.
4) Read your Bible and underline every promise of God that you read.
5) Listen to encouraging words. When someone gives you a compliment, accept it and believe it.
6) Don't let yourself think in absolutes, such as, "always," and "never."
7) Participate in activities that cause you to laugh.
8) Start speaking positively to yourself about yourself.

Successful Coping Skills

Coping refers to the ability to handle or deal with an issue. In many cases, coping is the ability to ride out the storm or to endure. See how many of these can help you be a better student.

• *Maintain an attitude that things will work out.* Envision the problem coming to an end. Anticipate the day when the problem will be resolved or the illness will come to an end.

• *Refuse to give in to negative thoughts and emotions.* Each time you have a negative thought, such as "I'm just a loser," replace it immediately with a positive thought. Voice these thoughts aloud. Say, "I am going to succeed," "I am going to learn something from this."

• *Put the past behind you.* You may have been responsible for the accident, been careless in a way that brought on the illness, or misjudged or miscalculated in a way that brought about loss. Forgive yourself for making mistakes.

• *Stay active.* When we suffer a temporary setback, one of our first impulses is to sit down and have a pity party. The time comes when you need to get up, dust yourself off, and move forward.

Read the Scripture passage below then complete the exercise that follows:

"Seeing then that we have a great High Priest who has passed through the heavens, Jesus the Son of God, let us hold fast our confession. For we do not have a High Priest who cannot sympathize with our weaknesses, but was in all points tempted as we are, yet without sin. Let us therefore come boldly to the throne of grace, that we may obtain mercy and find grace to help in time of need."

--Hebrews 4:14-16

Below you will find the Hebrews passage again...but this time with words missing. Fill in the blanks. If you need to review the Scripture again, that's OK.

"Seeing then that we have a _____ High Priest who has passed through the _____ , Jesus the _____ of God, let us hold fast our confession. For we do not have a _____ Priest who cannot sympathize with our _____ , but was in all points _____ as we are, yet without _____. Let us therefore come boldly to the _____ of grace, that we may obtain _____ and find grace to help in _____ of _____."

Perhaps as a student we aren't interested in the "throne of grace," but we can relate to "help us in our time of need."

How could this "affirmation" affect your relationships on campus? Below you find an acrostic. Use each letter to begin describing how God's affirmation impacts your relationships on campus. See if you can find a word or phrase for each letter. Be specific!

A _____

F _____

F _____

I _____

R _____

M _____

A _____

T _____

I _____

O _____

N _____

What benefit is it to you to know that Jesus has been tempted in every way?

_____

_____

What two things will we receive when we approach the throne of grace?

1. _____

2. _____

Summarize in your own words how receiving mercy and grace help us respond to the winning edge in a campus setting. (For example, I may not be as critical of my roommate when he or she doesn't do things the way I think they should be done.) _____

_____

Brent Price was drafted by the Washington Bullets in the second round. At 6'1", 175 pounds, Price was a high-scoring guard for the University of Oklahoma. But in a matter of a few days, Price was traded to the Houston Rockets. "My career has not been one that's been paved with gold. It's been rocky," he said. "It's been one obstacle after another, but I think that makes it much sweeter when you reach a point like this."

"My journey took me to the University of South Carolina and then to the University of Oklahoma. I struggled to make it in the NBA, and then there were the injuries––there were just so many obstacles," Price said, recounting his college travels and his NBA trials. "I never ever thought my ship was going to come in."

"As far as the team, the outlook of my career, and the position I'm in, I couldn't be happier. God's truly blessed me. God's grace has been good, and He has allowed me to be in this situation for a reason. I want to honor Him with that. There's no way I could have ever predicted, guessed, or hoped to be in the situation I am right now."[1]

A few years ago, Price was ready to give up on his NBA career. He was sitting on the bench as a third-string guard for the Bullets. How are you handling your personal setbacks? Do you give up and quit or do you seek God's help and move on? Like Brent Price, you can honor God in any situation you are in.

When I experience a temporary setback today, I will_____

Steps to Discovering the Winning Edge
1. Develop coping skills that will get you through minor setbacks.
2. Sand traps, minor setbacks, lack of organization, bad habits, and depression do not have to be a way of life for me.
3. Jesus was tempted as we are and has provided a way out.

Back 2 U
How would you describe Brian's setbacks?
What are some setbacks you have dealt with on campus?
If Brian were your close friend, what would you do?
What coping skills are helping you to discover the winning edge?

[1]Tush, Terry. "Rocket Man." *Sports Spectrum*, December 1996, 9.

Day 5: Enduring to the End

Principle: Endurance wins over temporary setbacks.

Lauren has entered her freshman year of college having never really finished a complete season on any tennis team. In her sophomore year in
high school, her dad was transferred during the third week of the season. During her junior year in a new school, she quit the team because
her grades were dropping, and during her senior year, she was projected
to be an all-district selection when she broke her arm during a match.
Lauren is committed to complete the entire year on the freshman tennis
team. There is no stopping her now.

With her present attitude, do you feel Lauren has the drive to endure to the
end of the tennis season? Check one of the following:
❏ Yes   ❏ No   ❏ Maybe

Lester M. Alberthal, Jr., is president, chief executive officer, and chairman
of the board of directors of EDS (Electronic Data Systems Corporation).
Founded in 1962, EDS today has revenues of almost $10 billion and profits
in excess of $800 million. More than 80,000 employees serve customers
in more than 35 nations. The company is an acknowledged leader in the
information business, specializing in how information is created, distributed,
shared, enjoyed, and applied. EDS is unabashedly gunning for the unofficial
title "World Technology Leader."

It's hard to believe that a successful person like Les Alberthal became president and chief executive officer of EDS in 1986 and was elected chairman of
the board of directors in 1989. He is widely recognized as one of the top exec-
utives in the world.

A more detailed account of his life is presented in the book, *Winning
in the Land of Giants* (pp. 184-186). One of the realities of life for Les
as he struggled to become the person God wanted him to be was that he
faced insurmountable obstacles, both personally and professionally. Yet, he
endured to the end.

Les knows that our life is a pilgrimage in which God speaks to us along the
way. Within his pilgrimage, Les has discovered eight principles he contributes
to his success in life and as a Christian.

Qualities For Success
(Based on the life of Les Alberthal)

❏ 1. He never separates himself from the basic family,
Christian, and personal values of his childhood.

❑ 2. He makes positive principles a habit.

❑ 3. He builds his tomorrow on the successes of today and yesterday.

❑ 4. He has learned how to motivate himself by being his own critic and then developing positive action steps for the negatives he sees in his life.

❑ 5. He has been willing to pay the price for success.

❑ 6. He surrounds himself with those things that renew him.

❑ 7. He genuinely seeks to help others.

❑ 8. He doesn't give up.

Examine these eight qualities. Could they "mirror" what you are beginning to experience as you seek to discover the winning edge in your life?

Go back to the list and put a ✔ in the box for qualities you see in your life. For example, you genuinely seek to help other people even as a student. Put an ✘ in the boxes where you know you need to grow. For example, if you don't often surround yourself with things that renew you, put an ✘ in that box.

Read James 5:10-11. Whom does the writer of James suggest that we use as an example of suffering? _____

_____

What examples did the prophets show?_____

_____

Who are considered blessed? _____
Why is Job used as an example? _____

_____

How does God respond to those who persevere? _____

_____

What does the experience of suffering do for the believer?_____

_____

_____

Paul writes to Timothy some encouraging words in 2 Timothy. Writing from prison, Paul affirms Timothy's strong faith and encourages him to be committed to Christ. He offers Timothy clear, practical advice and warns him of coming persecution. Paul emphasizes to Timothy that he should be faithful to the Word and preach it. If Paul was to write an encouraging word to you, now, what would he say? How would you want him to

respond to your own struggles? *In the space given, write the encouraging words Paul would say to you.*

Michael Jackson, pastor of Bethel Assembly Church in Rapid City, South Dakota, says we should consider some of the key figures in the Bible and examine ways they endured to the end:

- Moses could have easily given up. He had a bad crime on his record, a physical handicap, and a temper. But he didn't give up.
- Joshua could have said, "We've failed to enter into the promised land once. We have wandered around this wilderness now for 40 years––I quit!" But he didn't.
- Daniel, after having been a slave and having been tossed into a lion's den, could have said, "Everyone is against me. The king is trying to kill me. They don't want me to pray. Why, even the lions won't have anything to do with me. I'm done!" But he didn't.
- David could have cried, "I am never going to get it together. Why try?!" He could have easily given up. But he didn't.
- Peter might have said, "After what I have said and done, what's the use! I quit. Count me out!" But he didn't.

None of these great heroes of the Bible quit. They always accepted and fulfilled the new challenge put before them.

Of the five biblical leaders, to whom do you most relate and why?

How can a Christian make it when there seem to be no other believers around? Rob Pelinka was the sixth man on the Fab Five-dominated University of Michigan basketball team. Of his situation, he testified, "I was used to being surrounded by Christian people back home, and all of a sudden, I was at this huge university. There was no one to turn to with my problems, no one to share my joys. That's when I started walking in a personal relationship with Christ. I began to pray to Him as a friend and companion. My relationship with Him has just blossomed ever since."[1]

Rob Pelinka is an example of how you can stay faithful even when you are the only Christian around. He is "enduring" to the end.

I need to endure to the end this week by _____

_____

_____

Steps to Discovering the Winning Edge
1. When faced with adversity, look inward to your Christian values.
2. Practice and dedication take a lifetime to develop fully.
3. When pressured from others, stay faithful
and committed to the Lord.

Back 2 U
Why was Rob Pelinka able to experience change in his life?
In what ways could Lauren's determination be a positive element in her life?
When you think about the five people referenced from the Bible,
do you think they had discovered the winning edge?

[1]Egner, David. "Standing Alone." *Sports Spectrum*,
February 1995, 11.

Developing an Active Faith

Day 1: Taking the Blows

Principle: Active faith demonstrates God's influence.

Verse to Memorize This Week: "Not that I have already attained, or am already perfected; but I press on, that I may lay hold of that for which Christ Jesus has also laid hold of me."--Philippians 3:12

> Amanda was accused by another girl on her hall of taking some money from her room. The resident assistant became involved along with the dean of students. Amanda's parents were even called. After a few meetings, the accuser admitted she had made up the story because Amanda was asked out by her ex-boyfriend. A week later, Amanda saw the girl and told her she had no bad feelings for her. The girl asked for forgiveness. Was Amanda living out the winning edge?

What always happens in a boxing event. Both opponents get hit! Every Christian needs to know how to take a hit, because all Christians get hit! There's no way to avoid it. In taking a hit, the important thing is not whether you fall down, but whether you get up and come back strong. Oftentimes, it may seem that as a Christian student on campus, you are out for the count. There's no getting up when you are accused of being a religious bigot because you believe in Christian values. There's no getting up when you tell your roommate you aren't going to have drinking in your room. You might as well go down for the count! Wrong! *That's not "discovering the winning edge in your life!"*

When you are hit, give yourself some recovery time, but then get up again. You may have to go back to the dorm room and pray alone or with another Christian friend. Expect to strike a winning blow once you are back on your feet. When you come to this point in you life, *you will discover the winning edge!*

How do the blows come on campus? How are you hit as a Christian student? Four of the strongest blows you will ever encounter are: 1)insults, 2)rejection, 3)false accusations, and 4)deliberate actions intended to destroy you. Each of these is a blow below the belt. Even though you are fighting fairly, the other person may not.

Let's examine each of these blows as we develop an active faith.

Blow 1: Insults
Those who insult you will attempt to undermine your self-confidence...your character...your behavior. They have no basis for God's view of who you are. As you discover the winning edge, insults are no match for the power of your Christian will. You can draw your strength from God's love and forgiveness to resist insults.

Think of one insult someone gave you this week. Did you insult anyone during the week?

Blow 2: Rejection
Millions of students on campuses are reeling from the blows of rejection. Rejection comes our way in all sorts of ways. In taking the hit of rejection we need to keep one truth at the forefront of our thinking: people may reject us, but God won't.

God never rejects a person for who she is. God created us individually and loves us as His creations. We are His friends. He longs to communicate with us and have a relationship with us. God does not reject His children.

Identify a time you were rejected. How did it make you feel? Do you feel God rejects you as a person? Check one of the following.
❏ Yes   ❏ No   ❏ Sometimes

Blow 3: False Accusations
From time to time, others will accuse you falsely. Jesus taught that when this type of persecution comes for His name's sake, you are to rejoice. When you are falsely accused for your faith or accused for what you believe to be true, take the hit and roll with the punch. God has a reward in mind for you.

Check the type of accusations you hear the most on campus being used by fellow students. You are:

❏ worthless   ❏ stupid
❏ a failure   ❏ a cheater
❏ a dishonest person ❏ a party pooper
❏ a religious bigot   ❏ intolerant
❏ narrow minded   ❏ mentally slow
❏ destined never to graduate

Blow 4: Deliberate Actions Intended to Destroy You
Some students are intent on destroying you. If this is the case, they can nearly always find a way. They may seek to destroy your character, your leadership, or your faith. In either case, the end result is that you feel that you are a person with no worth. Don't allow this to happen. Check out God's promises: (Rephrase these promises in your own words.)

Revelation 2:7_____

_____

Revelation 2:1_____

_____

Revelation 2:17_____

_____

What are the four "hits" again? Write them in the space below.
1. I_____
2. R_____
3. F_____ A _____
4. D_____ A_____ I_____ to D_____ Y_____

Notice how the "four hits" we face from our fellow students and others compare to what we experience because we are Christians. Wow! We are the firstfruits of all He created.

The "crown of life" (see Rev. 2:10) will be given to believers who love the Lord more than their own lives and who live for Christ at all cost (see Matt. 16:25). This is your reward.

**Be one who discovers the winning edge.
Be an overcomer!**

Desmond Armstrong was a starter on the United States Soccer Team during the 1990 World Cup. From early 1993 to the spring of 1994, Desmond devoted himself to practicing and playing for the United States National Team. Because he was a promoter of soccer, especially in the inner cities, Desmond was one of the most recognized players on the team.

A little more than a month before the start of the 1994 World Cup, Desmond was cut from the team. He had been instructed by his coach not to pray for individuals before games and not to have Bible studies with his teammates in his home. These activities perhaps led to his release.

"God has a plan for me," Armstrong said. "If this is not the plan for me to be on the 22, that's when your faith is tested. I prayed when cuts were coming up for the strength to handle any decision. I can lean on the grace of God: He's in control."

"God is working out His plan for my life. I have to hold on. It's a test of faith. I pray that I've had a good testimony for Christ on the U.S. team. I hope I've demonstrated His love," Armstrong said. "I wouldn't change one thing. I am proud of living for God. I'm proud of being a child of Christ. I won't deny Christ for anything."[1]

There is a reward ahead! You will achieve the winning edge in your life!

We are to trust in what Jesus has done for us. We are to speak the truth about the Lord and about our relationship with Him. And we are to have courage. We are called to be people capable of taking a hit, and yet staying in the fight, all the way to the final bell––no matter how big the giant that is thrown in the ring with us.

Today, I will take the blows by _____

_____

_____

Steps to Discovering the Winning Edge
1. Never carry an insult in your heart.
2. God never rejects a student for who that student is.
3. Faith allows us to work through trials in such a way
that something good comes from them.

Back 2 U
Have you been in a situation similar to that which
Amanda was facing in the case study? What did you do?
Can you find a new direction in this session to help you
discover the winning edge?
Are you interested in a "reward" for Christlike living? It's yours!

[1]Gordon, Bob. "What Happened to Desmond?" *Sports Spectrum*, August 1994, 30.

Day 2: Teamwork that Works

Principle: Active faith demonstrates God's influence.

> Matt has played organized sports throughout college. He is considered to be a team player by all of his basketball coaches. Matt is unselfish in his play. He gives all he can in every practice, and he is a good student of the game. Matt knows that what he has accomplished he owes to the team. Matt's favorite saying is, "None of us is as good as all of us!"

We don't play the game of life on our own, although we may think we do. We can't do what we do without the help of a great many other people, some seen and some unseen. We are on a team whether we want to be or not. And as team members, we have obligations to the team. To experience the winning edge, it will only be done through teamwork.

TEAM OBLIGATIONS
Stay in the Game

1. Do Your Part to Reach the Goal
Teams must have goals to stay together. Sometimes these goals aren't spoken, and when that happens, team members often get fuzzy about where the team is headed and why. Jesus wanted us to be clear about the rules and directions we are to follow as His disciples. That's why we have the Holy Spirit, God's Word, and the church.

Teammates stick together. They help each other when the going gets tough. This is especially true when we face spiritual issues in life. Every Christian should be doing his or her part. The team depends on it.

2. Get Over the Loss
Even the best teams lose a game occasionally. That's life. Nobody has a perfect day everyday. When a loss occurs, the team must rebound immediately. The team that continues to focus on last Saturday's loss isn't going to be ready for next Saturday's game.

Individual players on a team sometimes give bad performances. Companies lose bids for concessions on campus. You need a new roommate. Your best friend will transfer to another school in order to get a better curriculum. You can't go with him or her! Be thankful for the time you have and move on to new friendships or new opportunities. Don't mope over what is done and let it control your thinking in a negative way.

3. Stay Loyal to the Team

Don't leave your team because you have a bad game or because you lose a game. Just because everyone hasn't memorized all the memory verses in this book is no reason for you "rag on them." Simply because some people come to a Bible study and they aren't prepared, doesn't mean you kick them out. Stay loyal to your Christian friends (who will make mistakes and let you down), your church, and your relationship with Christ.

Too often groups break up because they have gone through a tough time. Commit to the other students and strive to survive the tough times. Stay in the game. Nearly always, those who leave a Christian fellowship have at least a few moments when they wish they hadn't. No relationship is perfect. You are only trading in one set of struggles for another.

What would happen if you found a college church and made a commitment to stay there while in college? Think how much you could contribute to the body of Christ as you use your special giftings and abilities within the church. Every student has a place in the church. Stay in the game.

Use the acrostic to describe attributes of a student who is loyal to a Christian team:

L _____

O _____

Y _____

A _____

L _____

4. Play by Team Rules

All teams have rules regarding team behavior. No coach lets her team members do whatever they want to do whenever they want to do it, and then show up on Saturday to play. If a person is going to be a part of a team, she is going to have to show up for practices, follow instructions, eat the right things, do the full workout, and make the necessary grades. Team life is disciplined. The reward is play-time in the game.

List three positive behaviors which can take place when someone plays by team rules.

1. _____

2. _____

3. _____

Does this type of behavior belong to one who is discovering the winning edge in life? ❏ Yes   ❏ No

110

5. Hold Up Your Team Honor

Uphold your team honor even when you are out of uniform and off the field. Many students are critical of Christians because they seem to say one thing on Sunday and do the exact opposite on Friday and Saturday nights. Be faithful to your Christian friends when you are away from them on campus. Encourage other students to attend your church if they don't have a church home, and speak well of those who worship with you. We bear the name of Christ 24 hours a day, not just when we sit in a pew. We are members of the Lord's team wherever we go.

Read about teamwork in Philippians 3:12-21. Even as a college student, you are a member of this team. You can press on. You can reach the high calling. Don't let your team down!

Picture yourself as a starting member of a team. (The type of team is not important. Any team will do.) You have just finished playing a game. Your team barely lost. You played OK. The coach speaks to the team in the locker room and challenges each of you to play harder next week. His speech could have come from verses 12-14. What you hear from the coach is: (Put a ✔ in the box for all that apply):

- ❑ see you next week
- ❑ good performance
- ❑ proud of you
- ❑ you're pathetic
- ❑ did a great job
- ❑ you're losers
- ❑ played as a team
- ❑ don't come back
- ❑ we can do better
- ❑ trade
- ❑ keep up good work
- ❑ other_____

If the coach has committed herself to the winning edge in life, her response would be to build you up and let you know you are a part of the team...and sometimes teams lose. It's OK.

Jackie Slater was drafted by the Los Angeles Rams in 1976. As an offensive lineman from Jackson State University, Slater enjoyed three decades of professional football.

"I think it's been by the grace of God that I've been able to play so long with so few injuries," Slater said. "More than anything else, I have tried to do all the right things, and I've tried to take care of my body—lifting weights and working out with consistency both during the season and off season. Keeping in shape is always a top priority, even more so the older I get."

"With all of the success I have had and with the number of games I've played, I don't think those things just happen. I think those things were ordained by God for me to be playing with great ballplayers, to have such great coaching, and to play physically fit for so long. I think that this was God's will for my life as a

football player, and I have been truly blessed."

"I know what my role is as a player, and that is to give my quarterbacks and running backs the best protection possible," Slater said. "I have an opportunity to help keep them healthy and to see to it that guys like Eric Dickerson and Jerome Bettis and Cleveland Gary and Charles White have good statistical years. It's just a real joy to be a part of all that."

"They say that you measure a man by what he is able to do for others or by what he has done for others. If that is the measure of a man, then I really feel good about my career because I have been able to help so many people as a player."[1]

When we come to the final days of our lives, many things won't matter. What will matter is who we have become. What will matter is how you handle your relationship with Christ.

The choices we make nearly always affect other people. In fact, it is difficult to make a choice that doesn't touch another person's life in some way.

Keep your team in mind when you make life's choices, and ultimately keep in mind our Team Leader, the Lord Himself. He is the One who makes the team rules. He is the One who lines up our opponents and sets the schedule and gives us our dreams and desires. He is the One who organizes the members of the team and asks that we be loyal to them and to Him. He is the One who will evaluate our performance. And, most of all, He has the winning game plan. Guaranteed!

To demonstrate my teamwork, today I will _____

_____

Steps to Discovering the Winning Edge
1. Teammates stick together and rebound from losses.
2. Teammates are loyal, play by the rules, and uphold the team's honor.
3. None of us is as good as all of us.

Back 2 U
How is Jackie Salter's attitude part of the winning edge?
What could you do with other Christian friends to
show the campus that God loves them?
In what ways has Christ demonstrated the winning
edge in your life?

[1]Hunter, Kevin. "Ram Tough." *Sports Spectrum*,
February 1995, 23-25.

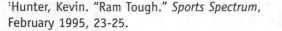

Day 3: Investing in Others
Principle: Active faith demonstrates God's influence.

Chris sat up most of the night listening to his roommate share about family problems back home. He didn't say a great deal, but his listening communicated the love and concern he had for his roommate. As his friend was talking, Chris was reminded of the words his uncle once told him--"God gave us two ears and one mouth. Maybe he expects us to listen twice as much as he expects us to talk." Chris continued to listen. Only briefly would he offer comments when asked.

Whether we want to or not, whether we mean to or not, whether we think about it or not, we leave an imprint on every person we meet. This is what happens when you discover the winning edge!

Name someone who has left a positive imprint on your life. Write that person's name in the space below.

Describe one reason you feel that individual left his or her imprint on your life? _____
_____
_____

Can you list at least three positive qualities this person demonstrated through his or her actions to you?
1._____
2._____
3._____

One person who made a positive imprint on me was Harry Earl McNeil, one of my college professors at Birmingham Southern College. I was not the least bit interested in taking college preparatory courses in high school, and as a result, when I entered college, I wasn't the least bit prepared for taking a course such as a foreign language. (Let me add, when I entered college I had a full-time job, a wife, and a family...and for some of the students I shared classes with way too old to be in college.) When I learned that I had to have two years of a foreign language to graduate, I nearly panicked. I didn't see how I could ever hurdle this barrier.

Through my involvement with the Baptist Student Union, I met Professor McNeil. He was the faculty sponsor for the BSU, and we came to respect each

other a great deal. He admired my stance against alcoholic beverages and my devotion to my wife and son. (I served in the military and then entered school after marriage.) I respected his boldness in standing up for God.

Professor McNeil became Señor McNeil, my Spanish professor. As I had expected, I struggled in his class. He kept telling me not to be afraid of being successful in Spanish, but I was too filled with grasshopper mentality at the time to believe him.

It wasn't something that Señor McNeil said, but something that he did that turned the tide for me. He invited me to come to his house every Thursday to eat pancakes and study Spanish. I spent Thursday nights in his home for two years, and in the process, I learned Spanish and passed the required courses. We also built up the attendance of the Baptist Student Union in those two years. We enjoyed a win-win relationship. In my estimation, Professor McNeil is one who has discovered the winning edge.

Life Investments Toward Discovering the Winning Edge

As you discover the winning edge in your life, here are some suggestions on how you can invest in others.

- Offer steady encouragement, believing in a person's potential and good qualities to take her to success.
- Put words to actions and help a person walk the walk to success.
- Model behavior that a giant slayer can be and should be a person of high moral standards of faith in God.
- Give something extra to somebody else and never expect anything in return.
- Model 1 John 4:11 when it says, "Beloved, if God so loved us, we also ought to love one another."

Our words must be consistent with our actions. Our lives are living testimonies to a mighty God. Our words can leave long-lasting impressions on others.

You have to be kidding! As a college student do you expect me to believe that this is instruction for "me?" I'm not old enough to do these things! Can you see a grasshopper around?

A Personal Investment

God has a plan for you and me. We are not to sit idly by and watch the world go to pieces. Rather, through our imitation of Him, we take the good news of the gospel of Jesus Christ to the world. No one needs to experience damnation! We have the opportunity to make an investment in the lives of others around us. As we are "salt and light," they will see in us a difference that is attractive to them. Your witness can

change their lives. They too will have the opportunity to discover the winning edge in life.

This is a time for personal reflection. Stop and think about what you have learned through this study. Now, what can you teach (invest in) others? In the space below write down two things you hope to invest in the lives of others.

Roommate(s): _____

_____

_____

Professor(s): _____

_____

Other students: _____

_____

Friends: _____

_____

Family: _____

_____

What you invest in people will be passed on to others as well. Years ago, a Sunday School teacher shared Christ with one of the young men in his class. This young shoe salesman received Christ in his life. At first his church did not accept him, because he was not educated. A full year later, this shoe salesman, D.L. Moody, became a member of the church. Moody became known for his Sunday School work in Chicago.

F.B. Myer, a pastor in England, invited Moody to his church to preach. Moody butchered the King's language and Myer was embarrassed. Moody told the story of a Sunday School teacher leading every person in his class to Christ.

Soon after Moody was in England, Myer talked with one of his Sunday School teachers and asked how she was doing. Her response was that because of Moody's message, she had won every child in her class to Christ. Myer became convicted.

Myer came to America to preach at a college. He met a student there who was ready to quit. With Myer's encouragement, Wilbur Chapman stayed in school and became an evangelist. Chapman needed a helper, and he found a former baseball player, a YMCA employee named Billy Sunday.

Sunday preached a revival in Charlotte, North Carolina,

in 1924. Depression came, and the revival fires cooled down. Some men got together and prayed for another revival. They invited Mordecai Ham to preach. During that revival, a 16-year-old farm boy gave his life to Christ. His name was Billy Graham.

You know the impact of Billy Graham's ministry. Do you know the name of that Sunday School teacher who shared Jesus with the young shoe salesman? Probably not, but his name was Mr. Kimble. Time will tell of the investment this one man made in the kingdom of God.

Investing in others. Who are you touching with your own life, in what you say or do? How can God utilize your total life?

To invest in others in a positive way, today, I want to _____

_____

_____

Steps to Discovering the Winning Edge
1. Your words need to be consistent with your actions.
2. Invest your life in others by giving encouragement and modeling high moral standards.
3. What you invest in people will be passed on to others as well.

Back 2 U
What do you think of Chris' approach to his roommate in the case study?
In what ways do you feel Christ is making a difference in your life on campus?
Do you feel Mr. Kimble (shoe salesman) ever thought he would discover the winning edge in life?
Do you feel this was a priority for him? Why or why not?

Day 4: Leaving a Legacy

Principle: Active faith demonstrates God's influence.

Shannon enjoyed just hanging out with her friends. This usually did not cost a great deal of money, which was good, since money was tight in her family. Shannon could be counted on and trusted as a friend. When she said she would pray about something, you could count on it. What Shannon's friends saw in her was the result of generations of love, support, and godly living. Just as important, Shannon's friends also saw the influence they had made on her life and her on their lives. Even in college, Shannon was developing and leaving a legacy for others to follow.

Your life is influenced by many other people and events over the years. Look at the list below and put a ✔ beside all which apply. As a student, what have you inherited?

❑ love   ❑ care   ❑ respect
❑ fear   ❑ dignity   ❑ lasting friendships
❑ achievement   ❑ failure   ❑ success
❑ mentors   ❑ new dreams   ❑ support from faculty
❑ career   ❑ faith   ❑ Christ
❑ procrastination   ❑ courage   ❑ spouse
❑ football games   ❑ second chance   ❑ winning edge

What would you add to this list?

❑_____   ❑_____   ❑_____

**The greatest legacy one can leave is a lifestyle
of consistency in word and deed.**

Winning-Edge Principles

Throughout school you are growing and developing principles which will direct your life. Below you will find six principles which come only as you understand your relationship to Christ and discover the winning edge.

Principle 1: A Student is Never Too Young or Too Old to Succeed

Winning-edge thinking doesn't come with maturity. Benjamin Franklin was a newspaper columnist at 16 and a signer of the Constitution when he was 81. Ted Williams, at 42, hit a home run in his last official time at bat. Mickey Mantle, was only 20 when he hit 23 home runs in his first full year as a major-league player. Mozart was only seven years old when his first composition was published. Age has little relationship to your ability to see yourself as a success and maximize your potential.

Principle 2: A Student Must First Accept His or Her Uniqueness as an Individual
When we concentrate on our uniqueness, we find our success. Ask yourself, What has God given me the ability to do? As you begin discovering the answer to this question, you are able to see beyond yourself. Then you have the ability to help other students discover what they can do best, what they desire to do, and what they are willing to work hard at accomplishing. See each student as an individual, and help that student see himself the same way.

Principle 3: Never Typecast Yourself by Your Outward Appearance or the Environment in Which You Grew Up
To think with the winning edge, learn to see yourself as God sees you: loved, equipped, and blessed. Examine your own potential and truly see yourself as a person created by God, destined for a purpose planned by God, and capable of being filled with God's Spirit to accomplish that purpose in your life. The fact you are in college is not a mistake. No matter what your home life is like, or where you grew up, God has a new plan for you. Begin anew and build on the lessons learned from the old.

Principle 4: Look for the Good and Praise It
When people do something we appreciate or value, we need to let them know it. We need to become "good finders." A fellow student helps you study for a test...someone offers you a ride because you don't have a car...someone shares their notes from class because you weren't able to be there...you have found a "listener." When we look for and find good in someone, we need to call attention to it. We begin by finding the small, ordinary, good things of each day on campus.

Principle 5: Positive Thoughts and Values Can Begin in a Moment, But They Develop Over Time
Consider the example of the Chinese bamboo tree. If you were to plant the seedling of a Chinese bamboo tree and water it and nurture it consistently, you might quickly become discouraged unless you knew about the growth cycle of this particular plant. There is no visible growth of a Chinese bamboo seedling the first year, the second year, the third year, or the fourth year. But during the fifth year, look out! The tree will grow nearly 90 feet in six weeks. Some people claim that if you stand next to a Chinese bamboo plant as it is growing, you can hear it snap, crackle, and pop.

Instilling positive thoughts and values into your life is like nurturing a Chinese bamboo seedling. We must stay after it and be steady in our words and behavior day in and day out, year in and year out. Growth will eventually manifest itself. If it's true for you, it's true for your friends and others on campus also.

Principle 6: Help Others Achieve Their Best Without Criticizing Them for Failing to Achieve Your Definition of Best

How many teachers expect all of their students to earn top grades? You know how unlikely this is. You may be a genius in chemistry, but your roommate is "slow" to say the least. Just making a passing grade is success for her. Her best may simply be passing the final exam with the lowest grade possible. She can be proud she passed and you can be proud as well...and tell her. She has done her best.

We all are guilty at times of wanting another person to achieve at a level that we have selected rather than being content to encourage her to do her best. Helping another person to be discover the winning edge requires that we help her identify her dreams, set her goals, make her plans, and defeat her giants.

Of the six principles listed, put a ✔ beside the one that holds the greatest influence for you. Put an ✗ beside the one you are still working on but desire greatly to influence how you live your life.

Imagine yourself an Israelite college student in the desert land of Arabaha, listening to the words of Moses. You are reminded of the time Moses selected leaders from among your tribes and how spies were sent to the country of the Amerites. You recall the grumbling in your tents thinking that God hated you and left you to be destroyed by the Amerites. You ignored God and were later chased down by the Amerites. Soon you began to conquer and possess the land God had promised you. Moses reminded you of other victories and how he spoke to God on your behalf. Then you heard God's commandments, given to you by His servant Moses.

Read Deuteronomy 4:9-14. What does Moses warn you not to forget? (v. 9) ___

_____

_____

What are you to do with what you have learned? _____

_____

_____

What instructions did God give Moses (v. 10)?

1. _____

2. _____

Based on how God has moved in your life and the lessons you have learned from Him up to this point, list three "instructions" you would most want others to pass on to students after you.

1. _____

2. _____

3. _____

Tom Osborn succeeded Bob Deavney following the 1972 season as head football coach at the University of Nebraska. Experiencing the highs of a national championship to the lows of players experiencing personal problems, Osborn has been a model of consistency and faithfulness.

"Whatever contribution I have made will be measured in wins and losses," Coach Osborn admits. "This is inevitable. The day after a coach is fired or dies, his record is printed in the paper." I suspect you could have won a lot of games but have been a very damaging kind of destructive type coach. You may have destroyed a lot of fragile egos and trampled on a lot of people at the wrong time."

"On the other hand, you may not have won that much but have made a tremendous contribution in the lives of a lot of people. Ultimately, the effect that you have on the lives of the people around you is the most important legacy you leave."[1]

What type of legacy will you leave? Will it demonstrate that you are a person who has discovered the winning edge in life? Will others know you have a personal relationship with Jesus Christ? Will they see you actively involved in Bible study, prayer, ministry, and in sharing your faith? This will, in fact, be determined by the life you now live. Determine now to leave a legacy worth passing on.

Because the winning edge is in my life, today on campus, I will _____

_____

_____

Steps to Discovering the Winning Edge
1. Our lives are influenced by many students and events over the years.
2. The greatest legacy we leave is a lifestyle of consistency in word and deed.
3. The legacy you leave will be determined by the life you now live.

Back 2 U
How was Shannon was leaving a legacy for other students
to follow by her actions?
What type legacy do you want to leave with other students
when you graduate?

[1]Erlandson, Doug and Elizabeth. "Leader of Men."
Sports Spectrum, September 1995, 11.

Day 5: The Winning Edge

Principle: Active faith demonstrates God's influence.

Robbie committed his life to the Lord at an early age, and is now planning to enter full-time Christian service. He occasionally speaks to youth groups around the city and is serving as vice-president of his BSU. Robbie prays everyday that the Lord will use him each day for His glory. He is excited about the opportunities for ministry which are opening up for him. Robbie is learning that there is no other way to live than to live for Jesus Christ. He is discovering the winning edge!

Write down three words or phrases that describe what "the winning edge" is all about for you.

1._____
2._____
3._____

The winning edge. It can come by way of a winning score in a game...an A+ on a test...an engagement ring...or any other action completed successfully. The winning edge, however, comes by way of submitting ourselves to the Lord's desires and allowing Him full and complete control of our lives.

Lesson from Nature
Have you ever thought about how a young eagle learns to fly? Probably not until today. That's OK! But there is a spiritual lesson to be learned from the eagle. The mother eagle has several steps she takes.

First, she gives her eaglets lessons about the power and capability of their wings.

Second, she shows her eaglets how to catch and ride the wind.

Third, she shows them the wind is their friend and they must learn to master the air currents.

Fourth, the mother eagle carries an eaglet on her wings and off they fly. Suddenly, the mother eagle swoops down and flings her eaglet in her wake. It's time to fly! It's time for the young eagle to soar on its own.

The Scriptures tell us that the Lord carries us as if we are on eagles' wings. He desires for us to soar--to fulfill our destinies. He desires for us to be more than conquerors, to be mighty men and women of valor, to be victorious in thought, word, and deed--both in the inner person and in outer achievements.

Living life with the winning edge is available to us because of who we are in Jesus.

Who You Are in Jesus

Read the following 21 Scripture references. Beside each Scripture is a letter of the alphabet. Match the letter of the alphabet to the phrase from the same Scripture. To get you started, I will do the first one for you.

Scripture	Phrase
<u>A</u> **Psalm 135:4**	____ I am a royal priest
<u>B</u> Isaiah 43:7	____ I am victorious
<u>C</u> Genesis 1:27	____ I am blessed with every spiritual blessing in high places
<u>D</u> Hebrews 2:7	____ I am the temple of God, the Holy Spirit dwells in me
<u>E</u> Romans 6:7	____ I am righteous
<u>F</u> 1 Corinthians 3:16	____ I am chosen for the Lord's own possession
<u>G</u> Galatians 2:20	____ I am crowned with honor and glory
<u>H</u> Philippians 4:13	____ I am forgiven through the blood of Jesus
<u>I</u> Titus 3:7	____ I am able to do things through Him who strengthens me
<u>J</u> 1 Peter 2:4	____ I am called by His name
<u>K</u> 1 John 3:7	____ I am a Son of God through faith in Christ
<u>L</u> Galatians 3:26	____ I am precious in His sight, honored and loved by Him
<u>M</u> 1 Peter 2:9	<u>A</u> **I am the Lord's treasured possession**
<u>N</u> 1 Corinthians 15:57	____ I am created in the image of God
<u>O</u> Deuteronomy 7:6	____ I am the one who has the mind of Christ
<u>P</u> Romans 1:7	____ I am an heir
<u>Q</u> 2 Corinthians 1:21	____ I am freed from sin
<u>R</u> Ephesians 1:3	____ I am anointed by God
<u>S</u> 1 Corinthians 2:16	____ I am a chosen generation
<u>T</u> Ephesians 1:7	____ I am called as a saint
<u>U</u> Isaiah 43:4	____ I am crucified with Christ, I no longer live but Jesus lives in me

Now, you are on your own to soar like the eagle from the illustration.

Read 1 John 5:1-12 and take one last look at how to discover the winning edge. Sharing your insights with friends on discovering the winning edge will be beneficial. Most of them will have no idea how to discover the winning edge in their lives. For them the winning edge may be financial success. To us, it's the truth in God's Word!

Who is born of God? _____

_____

What two actions demonstrate believers' love for one another? _____
1._____
2 _____

According to the Scripture passage, who are those who overcome the world? ___
_____
_____
_____

Who are those who are born of God?_____
_____
_____
_____

What are the four spiritual truths that are listed in verses 11 and 12?
1._____
2 _____
3 _____
4. _____

What determines whether you are living with the winning edge in your life
(v. 12)? Write it in the space below so you won't forget!

Cal Ripken, Jr., broke Lou Gehrig's streak of 2,130 consecutive baseball games
on September 6, 1995. During this time, his record will show he started every
game of his streak and played in 8,243 consecutive endings. That's playing
more than five years without missing an inning.[1]

A committed Christian and mentor, Ripken will no doubt be remembered for
these amazing facts. He will, however, also be remembered for the quality of
life he lived, a winning edge not only won on the field, but a winning edge
lived in his heart.

To celebrate the winning edge in my life, today, I will _____
_____
_____
_____
_____
_____

Steps to Discovering the Winning Edge

1. God desires for us to soar, to fulfill the purpose for which He created us.
2. Winning-edge living comes by way of submitting ourselves to the Lord's desires and allowing Him full and complete control of our lives.
3. Winning-edge living is available to us because of who we are in Jesus.

Back 2 U

What did Robbie do to begin discovering the winning edge in his life?
Can you think of a friend, family member, or classmate who does not live his or her life with the winning edge?
Can you help this individual discover the winning edge?

[1]Bentz, Rob. "Cal-culating." *Sports Spectrum*, November 1995, 20.

Discover The Winning Edge

Developing Powerful Positive Thoughts
Christ-controlled thoughts overcome inferiority feelings

Experiencing a Second Chance
God gives second chances to those who trust Him

Facing Life's Fears
Facing life's fears produces positive actions

Focusing on the Basics
Committed faith focuses on the basics

Winning Through Perseverance
Endurance wins over temporary setbacks

Developing an Active Faith
Active faith demonstrates God's influence

You have permission to make copies of the icons. You may want to put
them on a bulletin board in your room, keep them in a notebook you
use often or make copies for your friends. Let each icon remind you that
as we *Discover the Winning Edge*, it's a process. Return to the steps you
need for refresher at any time.

Additional books you may want to purchase and read

God's Invitation: A Challenge to College Students
by Henry Blackaby and Richard Blackaby

An interactive study specifically written for college students, this dynamic guide is based on the life of the apostle John. It focuses on the application of the seven realities of Experiencing God, and how these principles apply to collegiate life issues. You'll see daily decisions influenced as students apply God's invitation to their lives. Topics include (seven sessions):

- Seeing Your Life from God's Perspective
- Character: The Basis for Your Future
- Career: A Vehicle for God's Purposes
- Relationships: For Better or Worse
- Crisis: Your Moments of Decision
- Created for Interdependence: Living with God's People
- Kingdom Living: Getting the Bigger Picture

(ISBN 0805496793)

God's Invitation
Richard Blackaby & Henry Blackaby
Author of Experiencing God

Out of the Moral Maze by Josh McDowell
How do you determine values to build a lifestyle on?
Do you want values to last a lifetime? Josh
McDowell's *Right from Wrong* comes to life for college
students to help you through this interactive study.
It takes into account the fact that as you enter college
you face a culture that has lost its belief in absolutes.
In today's society, truth is a matter of taste; morality
of individual preference. *Out of the Moral Maze* interactive workbook will provide any truth-seeking college student with a sound moral guidance system
based on God and His Word as the determining factor for making right moral choices. Student workbook includes all teaching materials (eight sessions).
(ISBN 08054 9832 X)

Into Their Shoes: Helping the Lost Find Christ
by John Kramp and Allen Jackson
This new interactive study is designed especially for college students. It provides directions for building relationships with lost people and leads students to understand
the search for God from the non-Christian's perspective.
As "lostologists," students will learn to approach lost people with in-your-shoes empathy. Make a difference in how
many other students come to know Christ on your campus. Teaching suggestions included (six sessions).
 (ISBN 08054 9769 2)

Heaven: A Place To Belong by Joni Eareckson Tada
With this six-session study, now you can give college students a fresh perspective on the joys found
in being a part of the kingdom of God. Written by
the ever-inspiring Joni Eareckson Tada, it also
delivers new insights into what heaven might be
like. Perfect for collegians' schedules or retreat for-
mats, teaching suggestions for leaders are included,
along with clip art for your own promotion (six
sessions).
(ISBN 08054 9768 4)

To order—
- Write to the Customer Service Center;
  127 Ninth Avenue, North; Nashville, TN 37234-0113
- Fax (615) 251-5933
- E-mail customerservice@bssb.com
- Visit a Baptist Book Store or a Lifeway Christian Store